A Love Story—For My Children

To Father Richard Cartier

Sincerely,

"Ruth"

A LOVE STORY—FOR MY CHILDREN

Ruth M. Lester

iUniverse, Inc.
New York Lincoln Shanghai

A Love Story—For My Children

iUniverse books may be ordered through booksellers or by contacting:

iUniverse
2021 Pine Lake Road, Suite 100
Lincoln, NE 68512
www.iuniverse.com
1-800-Authors (1-800-288-4677)

ISBN: 978-0-595-46835-5 (pbk)
ISBN: 978-0-595-91126-4 (ebk)

Printed in the United States of America

Author's note

Names have been changed throughout this memoir in order to protect the privacy of individuals.

To Anna whose friendship is an inspiration, and to the memory of Edmund whose friendship made all things possible.

Contents

❀

Acknowledgments . . . .*xi*

Foreword . . . .*.xiii*

Chapter 1 1

Chapter 2 7

Chapter 3 12

Chapter 4 18

Chapter 5 26

Chapter 6 33

Chapter 7 39

Chapter 8 45

Chapter 9 49

Chapter 10 54

Chapter 11 59

Chapter 12 63

Chapter 13 69

Chapter 14 75

Chapter 15 80

Chapter 16 86

Chapter 17 91

Chapter 18 97

Epilogue *101*

Conclusion *103*

Acknowledgments

❀

There have been many times during my lifetime when I have felt the urge to put pen to paper if for no other reason than as a catharsis. Although my writing may have been a form of catharsis at its outset, it very quickly changed its objective. It has become instead an expression of the joy that is my life today—a tribute to all those I love so dearly.

These pages could not have come about if it hadn't been for the dogged determination of my children, John and Cindy. There are no words to express the wealth of gratitude this realization brings. But for their abiding love through all the years of uncertainty, my life today could not hold the same meaning.

To Jacqueline and James Michael—the children who blessed and enriched my life through all our years together—I express my heartfelt thanks for their generosity of spirit and their understanding, without which it would not have been possible to become the loving extended family we are today.

Special thanks to Gordon whose kindness and caring, in addition to his expertise and patience in editing my drafted meanderings, helped to make this book a reality.

Lastly, I want to express my thanks to Greg—the love of my life—whose support and faith in me and in my ability have prompted me to see this project through to its completion.

I can only pray, now that the work is finally concluded, that it may hold a thread of inspiration to be gleaned by someone in need of solace. If just one soul derives peace and resolution from the reading of my story, it will all have been worthwhile.

Ruth Lester

Foreword

❀

Every time I have read Ruth's story, from its first draft to its final edition, I have found myself emotionally affected. It's not just that my life has intersected with the players in Ruth's life history, but her story has a universal thread that tugs at the heart. It is the story of a woman whose life has been paralleled in other countries, cultures and societies. In fact, I doubt anyone can read her story and not think of someone they've known who went through similar experiences.

What makes Ruth's biography different is that her story has defied the odds: it has a happy ending.

Here is some background that will become increasingly relevant as you work your way through Ruth's book.

I come from a fairly traditional family background. My parents met during World War II when they were both working in Ottawa. My mother Faye, who left McGill University after her second year to help in the war effort, was supervising an office where tanks were designed. My father William had left the University of Western Ontario shortly before graduation. He was anxious to join his three older brothers who were in the services. At the time my parents met, William was a Captain in the Governor-General's Footguards. My maternal grandfather was stationed in the same regiment and he thought it would be a good idea for William to meet Faye and go on a date. Their initial meeting was a disaster and their relationship lasted a very short time.

But my grandfather's instincts were right. Several months later, my father returned for a second go-round and this time, the chemistry worked. Faye and William were married in May 1942.

William was the youngest of five children, a fourth-generation Canadian whose Scottish ancestors had backed the wrong side in Scotland's infamous Battle of Culloden. They fled to the Outer Hebrides for a couple of generations before heading to a brighter future in Canada. William was born and raised in London, Ontario.

Faye was the elder daughter of United Empire Loyalist stock (on her mother's side) and a dashing father who was born in Hereford, England, but who came to Canada as a baby when his family emigrated. Faye was born in Cornwall, Ontario, and raised in Cobourg.

When Faye and William married, they planned to have six children. Nature played some tricks, though, and they only had two babies of their own: my older brother Jason (called JM throughout his childhood) and me. I arrived less than a year after JM and there were complications during Faye's second pregnancy. After three subsequent miscarriages, my parents were told they could no longer risk Faye's life with another pregnancy.

That's when they decided to adopt. By this time, the war had ended and my parents moved to live in London, Ontario. My father went to work for a friend of his and JM and I began school there.

When I was barely eight years old, my parents told me that our family was going to increase: we were going to take in a foster child. This was the most delightful news I could have heard because they assured me that this new addition would be younger than I.

What glorious news. I could no longer be called the baby of the family because John was two-and-a-half years younger. What a relief.

A few days later, John arrived in our midst. All of a sudden, we were three boys instead of two and life became increasingly boisterous.

My parents had correctly used the term 'foster child' because we were not allowed to adopt John until a probationary period had passed. But once that day arrived, John was adopted with great ceremony. JM and I were both required to sign the adoption papers (this was my parents' idea, not a requirement of the adoption agency) and thereafter John was allowed to have *two* birthdays a year: his actual birth date and the anniversary of his adoption.

A couple of years after that, we moved to Woodstock, Ontario, where my father had bought a jewellery-and-gift store. We lived in a large house on a nice street, no more than two blocks from public school and high school, with our church just across from the school and the library at its corner. Dad's store was a five-minute walk away, and there were two parks within two blocks. We could bike anywhere safely and nobody locked their doors at night. This is what my friends now call our Norman Rockwell Childhood.

I remember that JM, John and I were away at summer camp when, quite unusually, my parents arrived for a visit. They introduced us to Anne, a six-year-old girl who was going to come live with us as the next foster child.

What an interesting change of dynamics it was to have a sister in our midst. I don't think we three brothers made Anne's life particularly easy, but essentially we had a happy childhood. Dad made a skating rink every winter in our back yard and we played hockey and had school skating outings. We were brought up with good values, lots of activities, in a lovely home with lots of space to play. Summers were spent at camp and at the family cottage, and lots of friends and relatives passed through our lives.

A few short years after Anne was adopted—and with the same ceremony that John's adoption entailed—our lives changed yet again. My mother's only sister had been diagnosed with what later was identified as ALS, now commonly known as Lou Gherig's Disease. Aunt Ellen and Uncle Joseph had adopted two babies from separate sources but my uncle could not look after them in Calgary while my aunt was in hospital in Montreal. Aunt Ellen had been flown to Montreal Neurological Hospital for treatment, so it seemed to make sense that my two little cousins come to live with us in Woodstock. After all, we had lots of room in our big, old house and what difference could two more children make?

So with the arrival of Anita and Tom, my parents' wish for six children had suddenly come full circle. There we were: six children from five different biological bloodlines. No two of us looked alike, thought alike, or appeared to be related in any way, shape or form. But we were a family and, for the most part, we remain so today.

And that's about all you need to know for now, as you begin to read Ruth's story. There will be more in a wrap-up Epilogue where Ruth and I will try to tie these stories together.

I'm sure you will find Ruth's story as touching as I have consistently found it to be.

Gordon Lewis

CHAPTER 1

❀

I had never seen so many boxes! There was still so much to be packed and yet there was no space left. How could the contents of five and a half rooms, once it was placed in boxes, take up more than its original space? I had already sold some of my furniture and had given away a number of items I no longer needed. My daughter Jacqueline was delighted to help me with the packing because it always meant going home with an armload of treasures. Still, there were simply too many items left and I had to make some drastic choices.

There were some things, however, I knew I could never part with—my father's cigarette lighter, for instance. Long ago it had been a vivid orange-coloured enamel, and now it was worn down to its brass base with only a dot of recognizable orange here and there. Every night when I went to bed, it was tucked under my pillow to help me drift off to sleep. In the morning when I awoke, both he and the lighter would be gone. I treasured that lighter just as I treasure the memory of my father—the father I knew as a small child, not the father of my young adulthood.

My mother was heavily sedated for the first hours following my birth. As a result, my father was the first to hold me—a few moments following my birth and at every possible moment thereafter. He adored children; he adored me.

Many babies are born with a shock of coarse black hair that is only tempo-rary. It soon falls out to reveal the infant's own silky colouring. I was one of those babies but, unfortunately, the hair had grown on my face as well. My mother was a very nervous and fearful woman at the best of times and, when she was finally able to see me, her first glance prompted a spontaneous nega-tive reaction that I believe established a life-long emotional space between us. Whether her reaction then caused me any sense of rejection is something for speculation. It is an accepted fact, however, that circumstance led me to bond with my father.

As an infant I'm told I cried all day, stopping only at the sound of my father's footsteps on the front porch at the end of his workday. Only then did I become a bundle of smiles. My earliest recollections are ones of absolute joy and delight—walking hand-in-hand with my father, riding high on his shoulders, or sitting on the living room floor with him to play games together. I remember watching him walk across that floor on his hands just to amuse me. When I was ill with whooping cough, he cradled me in his arms—holding me over layers of newspaper as my stomach heaved at the end of each prolonged bout of coughing. Although scarcely more than an infant at the time, I vividly recall that sustained, racking cough—a cough for which there was no cure but to run its course. Whether antibiotics might have been effective in curbing the violence of the infection matters not. Penicillin was yet to be discovered.

I remember, too, sitting in the crook of his arm as he held me up to touch the Christmas tree lights. I have a very clear memory of the night my father brought those tree lights home. It must have been Christmas Eve or perhaps a day or so before. I could see it was getting dark outside and there was a dusting of snow. I was standing in our front room waiting with eager anticipation. At last I heard footsteps on the porch and the front door opened. Into the room stepped my father—his arms laden with packages. He had been away working out of town as part of a hydro crew in Sarnia. My father's prolonged absence and my delight at his imminent arrival back home are probably what triggered that small snapshot of memory to be retained at such an early age.

Among the packages in my father's arms was a box of Christmas tree lights. What gorgeous lights they were! They bore no similarity to the modern Christmas tree lights. Among them were a bluebird, and a beautiful green and pink star. There was a clown and a Japanese figure in a colourful kimono. My favourite one of all was the Santa Claus face. I still remember the warm, satiny-smooth feeling of Santa's china beard when the lights were lit, and the contentment I felt nestled snugly in my father's arms as he held me up to touch the lights.

Those Christmas tree lights have always been my treasured possession despite the fact they could no longer be used. As the years passed, they grew brittle and increasingly fragile. Loving, almost reverently, I examined them once again before I carefully re-wrapped them in tissue, consigning them to the packing case along with all my other keepsakes. As I gently packed them there was no way of knowing that after all those years I would soon be parting with them.

Memories of my Christmas lights prompt memories of happy times during my childhood. Christmas was always a time filled with excitement. My parents' dearest friends were an Ohio couple who also had a daughter—Margaret. Margaret was eight when I was born and the close ties to her parents prompted my mother and father to give me Margaret as a middle name. Margaret's mother, Verna, was a robust and jovial woman who made me feel so very special. I basked in the warmth of Verna's attention, loving every moment spent in her company. I adored Verna—and Margaret as well—for Margaret also displayed much affection for me and seemed to genuinely enjoy sharing "grown-up" aspects of her life with me and telling me all kinds of "girl things"—just as I imagine a loving older sister would do. Margaret and her parents came to stay with us for a few days most Christmases. What joyful times those were!

Margaret's parents occupied my bedroom whenever they stayed with us, and Margaret and I would sleep together on the day bed in the front room. Sleep was actually not a very accurate description of our time spent on that day bed. We would whisper and giggle far into the wee small hours, always to the displeasure of my parents whose room was directly off the front room. The scolding we always received from my mother the next morning seemed part of the holiday ritual. However, my mother's ire did nothing to dampen our enthusiasm. Early afternoon we would all gather in the dining room for the long-anticipated Christmas dinner. The most memorable part of dinner to me was the whipped cream that topped our dessert—and the luscious red grapes. Christmas was the only day in the year they ever appeared on our table, and I loved them!

Christmas Eve was usually spent in Detroit at the movies. There was always a special stage performance of some sort in addition to the movie feature. Despite the fact that I loved going to the movies and loved being with Margaret, I was always apprehensive about the evening out. How could Santa Claus come to our house if we weren't home? We didn't have a fireplace with a chimney, so he obviously had to enter by the door—and if that door was locked …? Somehow, Santa always managed entry because each time we arrived back home to the sight of a tree laden with an assortment of packages. There was also one Christmas I recall that we spent in Ohio, and that clever Santa Claus even managed to find me there as well!

Of all the gifts Santa left, the one which stands out most vividly is that of a toy violin. Scratching the bow across the strings, I imagined myself creating the soul-stirring sounds I so loved to hear on occasion on our old Atwater Kent radio—the focal point of our entertainment in those days, long before the unimaginable television. The sound of a violin evoked a nameless passion that has remained with me throughout my life.

One Christmas, however, I remember that things were different. I'm not certain where it fit into the chronological order of things. My parents and I were sitting in the front room one evening when there was an unexpected knock at the door. My father opened the door to a man who handed him a large box and then quickly left. I have no idea what was said—I do recall my father's demeanour afterward. I would say that he appeared to be somewhat overwhelmed. The box contained all the makings of a Christmas dinner, and there was even a little doll for me. Most certainly there was a bag of the delectable Christmas hard candies that one would have to be of a certain age to remember. Just the thought of those candies brings forth a vision of Christmas. It's a pity they're no longer available although, in recent years, I have seen some candies that are similar in every way except taste.

I recall hearing my father recount the episode sometime later and I heard him say the Goodfellows had been our benefactor. All these many years I have remembered the name "Goodfellows" and only recently have I discovered that my memory served me correctly. The Goodfellows do indeed still exist. They are a charitable organization that still carries out fine work. We were apparently on the Goodfellows' list to receive the Christmas basket because we were on Relief at the time. Relief was the forerunner of today's Social Welfare.

One didn't have to apply for assistance in those days of Relief. I daresay Christmas baskets were distributed to our entire neighbourhood as a whole. It was a working-class neighbourhood—a working-class neighbourhood where no one worked. It was the time of the Great Depression—a depression that was great in scope only. It encompassed the entire Continent. It was a devastating time! Prices were rock bottom. Only a few cents could buy a loaf of bread, but who had a few cents? People grew vegetable gardens and kept poultry, cows and rabbits, and anything else they could raise for eggs or for slaughter.

We had a neighbourhood butcher who stocked a few shelves of groceries. The small shop provided whatever our own resourcefulness could not put on our dining room table at mealtime. A tab was kept of everyone's "purchases". No one had money but whenever any was forthcoming, the butcher received at least something on account. I loved the days when my mother was able to settle our bill at the store because it always meant a little thank-you item included in our bag of groceries. I particularly remember a cake—a beautiful cake with white icing, topped with a decoration celebrating the Coronation of King George V1 and Queen Elizabeth, more recently referred to as the "Queen Mum".

Although things were bad for us, it was possibly even worse in a number of areas. The West, which was always relied upon as the breadbasket of the Continent, was a dust bowl. The era was known as the "dirty thirties", an appropriate name for a time when men were reduced to the situation of hobo. Many a desperate man left his family behind and rode the rails in search of work—a boxcar to sleep in by night and a search for work and some food in whatever town daylight brought. Our house was only a couple of blocks from the railway line and it was quite a familiar sight for me to see a strange, shabbily dressed man sitting at our kitchen table having a plate of eggs with perhaps some tomatoes and a slice of bread or two. If my Dad was home at the time, the man might even be provided with a little tobacco for his pouch and a few cigarette papers. "Smokes" were rolled, not purchased in boxes done up in cellophane. The first packaged cigarettes I recall were in packs of five—the price for more would have been prohibitive. No matter how meagre the fare anyone could offer in those days, it was always deeply appreciated. There was an unspoken camaraderie that existed everywhere, for there was always someone who was in a worse state than your own.

At school it was quite normal for an inspector to come into the classroom, going up and down each row examining our shoes. Those with worn shoes were slated to receive new ones. At that time, inmates of Kingston Penitentiary were producing shoes. Trucks arrived at designated times and places in the neighbourhood where families would congregate to receive the clothing and shoes that were being distributed. My father brought me home a new pair of black oxfords once, as well as a dress. I remember the shoes but can't picture the dress.

Summer holidays were sometimes memorable, too. A variety of Ohio friends occasionally came to visit. Then I recall bottles of home-brew chilling amid blocks of ice in the bathtub. On occasion Margaret and her parents would make a summer trip to our house especially to collect me. They would take me back to Ohio with them for a week or so. Ohio equated absolute bliss as far as I was concerned. It meant spending many days and nights at Margaret's side, and all the while Verna doing her utmost to spoil me. I loved every moment of it! I remember one shopping spree where Verna bought me two new dresses, a new pair of white shoes, and a periwinkle blue felt hat. I was impressed with the shoes, in particular. My feet had grown considerably—several sizes, in fact, and had graduated from a child's size to a woman's shoe size. For the first time in ages, I could stand with my toes uncurled. Looking down at my feet, to me the shoes appeared enormous! Verna took a photograph of Margaret and me to send to my mother, and I'm wearing my newly acquired wardrobe. On the back of the picture Verna wrote, "You can even see the twinkle in her eyes." Whose eyes wouldn't twinkle?

CHAPTER 2

❀

I recall that at some point my young life changed very abruptly. I have never known why, nor have I any idea of the sequence of my memories. I vividly recall one hot summer's afternoon being so frightened that I slipped into the closet in my room, closing the door after me. I crouched in the darkness and tried to take shelter behind some bags of quilting scraps my mother kept stored there. I was terrified! I was certain that strangers who looked exactly like my mother and father were posing as my parents and they meant to harm me. I also knew it was all-important that I not let them know I was aware of this. I have no idea what prompted the idea that my real parents had vanished—or why I had so much to fear from these impostors—but as I crouched there in the dark I felt desperate. I had to escape somehow! I recall wishing with all my might that I could go back to wherever I had come from. In retrospect, since I was still unaware of the process of birth and the fact of death, I can only assume it was an unconscious wish to no longer go on living.

My heart was pounding as I heard my mother's footsteps approaching. Suddenly the door of the closet flew open and there stood my mother, admonishing me for my silly behaviour on such a hot day and insisting that I come out before I had heat stroke. I recall scrambling out of the closet and away from her before she could guess my thoughts.

I'm not certain whether it was around this time or later but, in any case, I made the decision to run away from home. I don't know what prompted the decision that particular day, but I do know I was still much too young to have any idea how to carry out the venture. I recall making a single sandwich to take with me because I knew I'd surely be hungry. I made no provision for rain or for cooler temperatures. I started out, just as I was, in a light summer dress and bare-footed with Toodles, my kitten, tucked under my arm.

Unaccustomed to being out on the street by myself, I walked in the only direction I knew. It was the way I walked with my mother whenever we went to the butcher's store. It was also the way to the railroad tracks my mother always crossed to reach the path, running along the far side, which eventually led to Memorial Park. The park had a wading pool and my mother sometimes took me there to splash around on hot summer afternoons. Otherwise, the sprinkler would be set up on our lawn and I would run with delight in and out of the spray. Bees were in abundance and I don't ever recall a day when I didn't get stung at least once while playing under the sprinkler.

I can now only recall that long before Toodles and I reached the tracks, she became very restless. Toodles began to squirm and it was difficult to hold her with my one free hand—I carried my sandwich in the other one. The sky had begun to darken, and a sudden storm appeared imminent. This probably accounted for Toodles being so ill at ease. The severe summer thunderstorms in our area caused frequent lightning strikes on and around our house. I don't recall being frightened by the ominous clouds, but Toodles obviously knew what was best for us, so back home we went. I have no recollection of what happened after we returned. In all likelihood my mother was so preoccupied with the advent of a storm that our absence from home had gone unnoticed. My mother was terrified of thunderstorms.

For whatever reason, as my childhood progressed, my father became an aloof stranger. At night, my parents fought. I would lie in bed and cringe—my head buried under my pillow in an attempt to drown out the sounds of their harsh words. I couldn't stand the shouting. It frightened me. So often I heard the word "she" and presumed it to mean me. I was undoubtedly a source of trouble to them and I felt miserable at the uproar my existence seemed to cause. At one point I distinctly heard my father say, "If you can't handle her, I'll leave." His words struck a note of fear in my young heart. The prospect of living without my father added greatly to my already existing anxiety.

I don't know when my mother began hitting me—or why. It seemed I was always taken by surprise. She would just suddenly pounce. For years afterward I had a fear of birds because of the way they swoop down unexpectedly. They reminded me of my mother who was tiny, always moving quickly, and "bird-like" in so many ways.

The beatings began with a cedar shingle that stung when it hit the backs of my bare legs. I recall being covered in purple welts and trying not to let anyone see me from the back. I also remember lying about the marks. By the time my mother progressed to using my father's razor strop, I had discovered that she felt some sense of satisfaction when I began to cry, or if I ran from her in fear. From that moment on I chose to deny her that satisfaction.

I also learned not to be startled when my mother suddenly came for me. I soon discovered I could somehow detach myself from sensation in a way that enabled me to stand unflinching and dry-eyed as the strop came cracking down again and again. The less I responded, the more frustrated she became. The more frustrated she became, the harder she struck—and the harder she struck, the greater was my determination not to give in.

Finally, when my mother's anger was spent, I would go quietly on with whatever I had been doing as though nothing had happened—denying her even that acknowledgement. I don't know what emotion she felt at this point but I always felt myself the victor. In the battle of wills, I was the winner. I had learned to hold myself intact, causing her to lose control, and this gave me some measure of satisfaction.

I don't know how often these beatings took place. Looking back, however, it doesn't seem reasonable they could have occurred beyond the span of one summer. In winter months I would have been amply protected with clothing. Girls my age wore long, thick, ribbed cotton stockings held in place by garters suspended from a belt fastened around the waist. This was the era before tights. Panty hose were also unknown, as were nylons. Women wore garter belts from which were suspended stockings made of silk, lisle or a cotton blend. Women, as well as girls, wore skirts. It was a time before slacks—only men wore trousers. Men also wore shirts and ties for virtually every outing from a picnic to a town-hall meeting. They wore shirts and ties, and suits. Most often they wore suspenders to support their suit trousers—the suspenders hidden from view by a vest. Hats were also an every-day part of a man's wardrobe—straws in summer; felt fedoras in winter, and caps for all seasons. Jeans in those days were worn strictly as work attire, and most often they were overalls. All clothing in those days featured button or snap closings. Zippers and Velcro were yet to appear on the scene.

Winter warmth in our home, as in most neighbouring homes, was provided by a coal-burning space heater in the front room. A wood stove in the kitchen provided heat for cooking as well as for comfort. I loved it whenever my mother simmered a pot of soup or boiled vegetables for dinner on a cold winter day. The most beautiful icy pictures would begin to appear on the kitchen windowpane as the warm condensation from the steaming pot on the stove met the frigid glass. I was told it was Jack Frost's handiwork. I never tired of gazing at his masterpieces and did my best to search out every intricate detail. In my mind's eye I can still see some of that glorious artwork to this day.

Bedroom temperatures were frigid, so dressing took place as close as possible to the front room stove. Permanently scarred elbows from daily encounters with that stove while quickly struggling into an undershirt were *de rigueur*. That same stove provided a routine summer chore because the coal fire produced a fine sooty film that settled on everything. The film wasn't all that noticeable until it was introduced to "Climax" wallpaper cleaner—a bright pink putty-like substance that came in a squat, round can with a navy blue and white label. When stroked gently across the wall, Climax left a remarkably clean swath that revealed just how much soot had accumulated over those cold winter months. The bright pink cleaner quickly absorbed and became the colour of soot.

At Saturday night bath time, warmth was provided by a small electric heater that consisted of a round reflector which housed a small white bakelite cylinder surrounded by a myriad of tiny little coils of wire. Kettle after kettle of hot water was heated on the wood stove and poured into the big round galvanized tub set up in the little area destined to one day become a bathroom. Daily bathing consisted of a quick sponge. Temperatures dictated that one remain fully clothed as much as possible. Under-the-bed chamber pots, or commodes, were the vogue in those years. A trip to the outhouse in the middle of a cold winter's night was something to be avoided. This added yet another chore to the long list for the hard-working homemaker to perform each morning.

Whatever the time frame of the beatings I endured, I can't bring myself to believe that my father knew of them. I do know that my father never struck me. Whenever my behaviour warranted his disapproval, a stern look from my father was more than sufficient to bring tears of remorse. I do recall him chastising me for whining—and on more than one occasion. I have no idea why I whined, or "belly ached" as he sometimes referred to it. I suspect it had something to do with my need for his affection and the unexplained sudden lack of it.

By the time I was eighteen I had only the pretence of a relationship with my parents. We lived together, the three of us, in close proximity under one roof yet worlds apart. Casual conversation was not a part of our family life, nor had it ever been. There had been no form of communication that would enable us to know or understand one another better. Whatever the reality was of the relationship between my parents, I can only surmise. Words spoken between the two of them, at least in my presence, consisted only of those of the utmost necessity. Perhaps they had a deep understanding of each other that rendered words unnecessary.

Despite the lack of communication in our household, my parents conversed quite freely with friends and neighbours. In the presence of others they seemed as two entirely different people and I'm not certain now that I was even aware of the seeming dysfunction within our family. I do know that I felt we were somehow "different"and that I was always envious of my friends who had siblings and routinely related anecdotes of a family life so far removed from my own. There was something lacking in my frame of reference that always prevented me from feeling akin to whatever it was my friends experienced.

In my heart, however, I always maintained my adoration of the warm and loving father of my early childhood. It was simpler to disregard our later relationship and to bury the feelings of abandonment triggered by his apparent rejection of me.

CHAPTER 3

❁

How to pack my photos! The albums didn't concern me as much—though I hadn't realized there were so many—but the framed pictures I had taken down from my bedroom wall would have to be packed very carefully. As I gazed at the heavily moustached men with their long sideburns and meticulously slicked hair, and the women in long, bustled dresses fitted over stiffly corseted figures, it was difficult to believe these could be members of my family—my ancestors. I could identify my grandparents from other pictures I had seen, but who were all these other people? As I looked at the faces of my kin, total strangers peered back at me.

It is understandable why I know so little of my forefathers. My parents eloped when they were very young, leaving their northern Ontario homes for a life in Fremont, Ohio. They lived there for seventeen years until my birth was imminent, at which time they returned to Canada.

My mother was the daughter of a Presbyterian Minister—a seemingly humourless man with an equally dour wife. Together they raised my mother under the most rigid rules. Some of those rules became all too familiar to me when I was required to sit quietly on a Sunday—having to forego running, skipping, and even laughter. The answer to any of my queries as to why I shouldn't engage in any particular activity on that day was always the same, "Because it's Sunday." Although the rules were strictly enforced, any explanation of their origin and any form of religious instruction were sadly lacking.

My father was the black sheep of his family—the youngest of many children—thirteen, I believe. It was presumably objection to my parents' union that prompted their flight to Ohio and their lack of contact with families back in Canada. Thus it was that I grew up knowing very little of my grandparents, and nothing of my father's large family. The only history I know regarding my father's ancestors was they had come from Ireland to Canada some four generations previously, and that my father's grandmother had lived in their home when he was growing up. I did hear my father relate a story to guests recalling what he had been told of his grandmother. She was a small woman who smoked a white clay pipe and carried sacks of grain almost as large as herself to the mill at York—site of the present city of Toronto. My father also recalled that as a child he had been fascinated with the rockers on his grandmother's chair and how they had worn thin with her years of daily rocking to and fro.

My mother did tell me that she once had a younger sister. Although I have no idea of her name, I do know she was a Down's syndrome child—what in those days was referred to as a "mongoloid". I cringe at the thought of my mother's description of her sister as having been "no good", explaining that she had lived in a kind of high chair until the age of eighteen when she died of dysentery. This sister does appear in one of my mother's photographs. I was also told that some of my relatives had died during the flu epidemic that blanketed the globe at the close of World War One. Few other facts regarding my parents' families were shared with me as I grew up, or even their own personal story for that matter, so all is now lost forever in the mists of time.

My parents did not register my birth. Why they didn't still remains a mystery. It also remains the cause of much speculation. I learned of the fact of my "non-existence" many years later when I applied for a copy of my birth certificate. Instead of a certificate, I received an application form accompanied by a terse note stating that I was not included in any records. My mother was furious with me! She would offer no explanation or response to my enquiries, nor was I allowed to see the completed application form. My mother took care to mail the form herself.

At the time, I thought perhaps my mother's actions came about because I had placed her in a difficult position—though unknowingly. I believe the form letter I received did make reference to a possible fine. Of this I can no longer be certain, and whether or not she did pay a penalty can only be speculated. Looking back, I am now more than a little puzzled. Was there a secret so important to her that she dared not disclose it, even to register my birth? I am not adopted—of this I am certain. Too many references were made throughout my childhood to various inherited physical attributes and, of course, there are the few facts I was told about my appearance at birth and my mother's poor physical condition at that time. I've had reason in recent time to search for records of my parents' certificates of birth, marriage, and any other pertinent information the Internet has to offer. No marriage document appears to exist although I do have records of both their births. I note that my mother's birth was registered when she was three months old, in 1894. This, for some reason, perplexes me all the more knowing that birth registration was a fact of life so many years previously. Could it be my parents never legally married, or did they marry only after they took up residence in Ohio? Such a situation in those days, especially for my mother and the extreme moral principles instilled in her, would have been sufficient reason for her to avoid disclosure at any cost.

Birth certificates were not an admission requirement in the days when I started school, nor was there a kindergarten. School began at grade one level at the age of six. Because I was tall for my age and could already read and count, my mother chose to enrol me into grade one when I had just turned five, instructing me to say that I was six. The manner in which my mother stressed the necessity of saying I was a year older than my actual age made it seem very serious to my mind. It was always a source of anxiety to me to remember how old I was supposed to be, for I dared not even disclose my real age to other children. Never once do I recall ever divulging my great secret to anyone.

I have always felt it was a mistake to enrol me in school so early. In reality, it was almost a year and a half early. As an only child who had no experience with sibling rivalry much less with the concept of sharing, I had trouble integrating. The other children played together so naturally. I had no idea of how to join in.

I had always been very sheltered—overprotected is probably a more adequate description. My lack of experience in relating to other children was compounded by the fact these were children older than me. I could only stand anxiously on the sidelines and watch, uncertain as to what was expected of me, either in or out of the classroom.

My birth was finally registered on August 15th, 1946, many years after the fact. With the arrival of my certificate came the reassurance of facts regarding my birth and what a blessed relief it was. This did little, however, to satisfy unanswered questions. Age in itself is not my enemy as I have a youthful manner and appearance, but self-doubt and speculation are. Why was it not important enough to register me at the time of my birth? Or what was it that could have seemed even more important? It was only years later that I was confronted by the realization I had never been christened or baptized, so no such records existed either.

The only place I was allowed to go by myself during my pre-school years was immediately across the back alley to play at the home of the Bartolli family. The Bartollis were an Italian couple who had immigrated to Canada and were raising several young children. One, a boy, was my age and virtually my only playmate. Some of my fondest childhood memories are of the simple pleasures I experienced in the Bartolli home.

Mrs. Bartolli was a warm and generous woman whose kitchen was always filled with wonderful aromas, the likes of which I never experienced at home. Although she spoke no English, Mrs. Bartolli always managed to communicate an air of warm welcome to me. The Bartolli children had a swing suspended from the overhead beams in their basement where we spent many happy hours. I can still recall the delicious smells of ripening cheese and fermenting grapes that would soon become wine. I remember too, the year Mrs. Bartolli baked a birthday cake for me and made me a pair of velvet slippers. I was often invited for dinner at the Bartolli home—possibly because I didn't leave when they were about to sit at the table. My mother, for years, thought I had the appetite of a sparrow because she couldn't entice me to eat at mealtime. I couldn't tell her I was already full of Mrs. Bartolli's scrumptious cooking because my mother's cooking left so much to be desired. She seemed quite content to allow me the "loaf of bread" made into sandwiches that I devoured just before bedtime most nights.

The Bartollis kept a Jersey cow called Bossie, and sometimes Mrs. Bartolli made ice cream from the cream that Bossie produced. Sometimes she roasted peanuts that she grew in her vegetable garden. One year they kept a pig—a sow obviously—because she soon produced a number of shoats, all of which escaped one summer evening. I watched on in amazement as the tiny pink bodies would be caught one by one only to appear to squirt right out of their captors' hands. I don't recall how they were finally rounded up, but I do remember the amusing spectacle their escape provided!

There was a new baby girl born to the Bartollis and I was fascinated as I watched the breastfeeding of the newest member of their family. I was awe-struck by the precious bundle Mrs. Bartolli held in her arms. Oh, how I longed to have a baby at our house! Mr. Bartolli was a kind man, although given to teasing. He suggested that if I had a dollar I could, indeed, have their baby. Before there was time to straighten the matter out I was across the alley in a flash, pleading with my mother for the dollar. I was so excited! My words were tumbling out in torrents and there was little room for her to respond. My mother began to laugh. My excitement dissipated, giving way to puzzlement. Didn't she want us to have the baby? She told me that Mr. Bartolli was just teasing me. I remember going back across the alley, embarrassed and crest-fallen. I don't recall how I was greeted when I arrived back there, but I do know

I never for a moment held any animosity in my heart toward Mr. Bartolli. We obviously patched things up satisfactorily.

In front of our house at the foot of Charlotte Street, we had a fenced yard with a gate. I knew better than to venture beyond that gate. Instead, I spent many hours swinging on it as I watched the neighbourhood happenings from my vantage point

Toodles, my cat, was my constant companion throughout my childhood. My father brought her home one day tucked inside the zippered front of his jacket. He had discovered her in a gravel pit where she had obviously been abandoned as part of an unwanted litter. He swung down from his bicycle, opened his jacket, and handed me my very own kitten! I had pet rabbits when I was a toddler and they appear in my arms in many of my early photographs. Although the rabbits were cuddly and followed me everywhere, they were not especially responsive to my petting. Toodles was different. She purred loudly and nestled herself against me as I caressed her.

Whether Toodles possessed some innate sense or was simply an unusual cat, she cared for me in a most unusual fashion. At the first sound of any crying, she would come bounding from wherever she might be. She would spring up and wipe away my tears with her tongue as quickly as they fell, all the while purring loudly and doing her utmost to comfort me. I recall one particular day when Toodles came to me meowing and circling me strangely. There was an urgency about her as she moved around me and then walked away a short distance only to return and circle me again. It appeared she wanted me to follow her and, when I did, she led me all the way up the path to the very back of our garden. There, in a box tucked behind the rabbit hutch, I saw her beautiful little still-blind kittens. It was obvious she wanted me to pick them up and, one by one, I did while she sat beside me purring as though to burst with pride. Her presence was my great comfort for all my growing years until the day she grew too old to go on living.

People tend to think of cats in general as independent creatures—friendly and playful only when they wish to be. Toodles was the great exception. It seemed as though her sole purpose in life was to please and comfort me. My cheeks still burn with shame when I think of the times I slapped and scolded Toodles for no reason other than to see her reaction. She would remain perfectly still—waiting, scarcely breathing. After a moment I'd pick her up and hug her and gently whisper, "I'm sorry, Toodles." Instantly she would spring to life purring loudly and snuggling close to me once again reassuring me of her devotion.

I can't help thinking Toodles understood how lonely and insecure her young mistress was, and how troubled by fears of abandonment. What a balm Toodles' love was to me. I sincerely believe her loyalty and lessons in selfless love played no small part in teaching me to trust.

Toodles lived to be quite old, and I watched as her body grew stiff and brittle. She was virtually toothless. Jumping down from any height caused her to land with a jarring thud. I vividly recall the summer afternoon my father brought Toodles to me out on the same front lawn where he had first handed her to me as a tiny, downy-soft kitten. He told me it was time to say goodbye. He had decided to have Toodles put to sleep. I understood the necessity as I cradled her in my arms one last time. Then, as I handed Toodles back to my father, one of her claws caught my finger. It was the first time she had ever hurt me. I watched my father's car pull out of the driveway, down the street and out of sight. Only then did I think to look at the scratch. It was deep and it was bleeding profusely. Even in parting Toodles had been my ally. She had given me a visible wound to fuss about so that I might hide my deep inner hurt and the overwhelming sense of loss caused by our separation.

CHAPTER 4

❁

For so many years it seemed my world consisted of our front yard. When I wasn't swinging on the gate, I was playing on the front porch. We had a large porch that ran across the entire width of our house, with trellises supporting an array of Paul's Scarlet climbing roses that burst forth each year in the most spectacular blaze of colour. The gorgeous deep crimson blooms made a startling contrast to the white clapboard of the house with its dark green trim and trellises. Cars made a point of driving past slowly—or even stopping—just to take in the amazing sight. It was from that porch at dusk that the Evening Star appeared directly ahead. Just off to the right was the red ball in the sky that perched atop Detroit's Penobscott Building—that city's tallest building at the time.

Only when I began school was I allowed out of that front yard. How large the world seemed to me then as I crossed the nearby field that lay between our house and the school! In summer that field served as a softball diamond and in winter it was transformed into a skating rink. Throughout all seasons it served as a pasture for Bossie, the Bartolli cow. In spring it was where I gathered wild mushrooms and baskets full of dandelion greens for my mother—and when they came into bloom, the dandelion flowers. The greens were cooked as a vegetable for our meals, but the flowers were made into dandelion wine. There was always a bottle of the yeasty smelling concoction resting against the block of ice in the top of our icebox.

Ice was brought around the neighbourhood on a daily basis, similar to bread and milk delivery. There was a card for each of the commodities and the appropriate card placed in the front window guaranteed delivery that day. I loved the day the iceman stopped at our house. He always chipped off some little pieces for me before lugging the big block into the house. Sucking on a piece of ice on a blistering hot summer morning was just about the best treat imaginable in those days. The iceman had a truck and so did the bread man, but a horse drew the milkman's cart. Silverwood's Dairy was known for its beautiful horses. They were show horses and every main event in the city featured Silverwood's horses going through their paces—all decked out with their pompoms and braid—and very much aware that all eyes were on them.

There was another cart drawn by a horse, but it only went by from time-to-time. It was driven by the Rags and Bones man. He would drive by our house calling out, "Rags and bones." I'm not certain whether my mother ever made use of his services—neither do I really recall what his purpose was. Perhaps it was to collect items that couldn't be readily disposed of. It's most likely he received money from recyclers who could make use of his collections. Garbage in those days was disposed of by individual households. Ours was burned in a large metal drum at the foot of our lot. My father had cut out appropriate holes so it could function as a furnace.

On the far side of the multi-faceted field that stood adjacent to our house was a wheat field. I had to cut across the corner of this field to reach the bungalow that housed the grade one classroom. In autumn after the wheat was cut I could see farm buildings away in the distance on the far side.

Our grade one bungalow was built beside another similar structure that housed grade two. After we had finished the first two grades we transferred to the low red brick building that housed the rest of the grades up to grade eight. After that, we were obliged to attend a high school a number of miles away.

The grade one bungalow was more than just a classroom. It was the building that was rented out as a hall for so many of the community activities. It was used by Brownies, by Girl Guides, as a meeting place for a Horticultural Group, for concerts, and even a Sunday school. I recall Keno evenings too, which my parents always attended with me in tow. My mother would never have dreamt of leaving me in the care of a baby sitter. I often managed to fill up my card with the dried kernels of corn provided—laboriously searching out the numbers as they were called aloud. Prizes were modest and practical. I recall we enjoyed a number of fine meals as a result of my winnings.

I loved school once I had gotten past the difficulties that recess posed. Unfortunately, my Bartolli playmates attended the tiny Separate school taught by the Nuns. I was truly on my own at the beginning of Public school. There was also the hurdle of arithmetic that caused me no end of distress. Although I could count before I started school, and knew all the numbers, I couldn't do anything with them. Numbers simply wouldn't add up for me, nor would they behave in any way as they seemed to for other children. I recall sitting at my desk crying—alone in the classroom except for the teacher. All the other children had gone home for lunch. We had an arithmetic exam that morning and I had answered virtually none of the questions to that point. I remember tearfully asking the teacher if I might be allowed to go home for lunch and then return to finish the exam. I have no recollection whatsoever of her response. However, I do know that my math skills scarcely improved from that time onward. Despite my inability to multiply and divide, however, I made good marks in other subjects. I skipped grade four, going directly from grade three to grade five.

I enjoyed doing homework. Parents didn't become involved with their children's school assignments in those days—possibly because in a lot of cases the child had already progressed to a level beyond that of their parents. In my case this was a blessing because homework represented something I could do completely on my own. It represented a kind of privacy and escape from supervision.

During the earliest years at school I seemed to form friendships with boys rather than with girls, despite the fact that boys and girls played in separate areas in the schoolyard and we had separate entrances. After school it was invariably a boy I brought home to play for an hour or so before supper. I had never been accustomed to girl's games. I didn't have much interest in dolls apart from seeing how it was their eyes opened and closed, or what material they were composed of, though I did enjoy cutting out paper dolls and their clothing. I liked playing cowboys or shooting marbles, building forts and making slides in winter whenever it snowed. We sometimes played games like Red Light and Hide and Seek—and there was always skipping and hopscotch. I amused myself by playing catch—bouncing the ball off the side of our house. I especially enjoyed acrobatics out on our front lawn—turning summersaults frontward and backwards, and cartwheels. Gradually, as I grew older, I began to have girlfriends—usually only one as a "best friend". Annie was the name of my grade school friend. However, there continued to be boys in the picture and this reality was most probably due to my fondness for the type of games they played. I enjoyed playing "scrub" on the school baseball field after hours and weekends. I couldn't catch and I couldn't throw a ball any distance, but I was a "slugger" and could always be counted on to bring in runs.

There was also a rather rough game called Jimmy Jimmy Long Tail that required the players to form two teams. One team of players had to form a "chain". The head of the chain would bend forward holding onto a post while the others lined up behind, bending forward with their arms around the thighs of the person ahead of them and with their heads neatly tucked in on one side. The other team of players then lined up a short distance behind the "chain" and each, in turn, took a running leap while shouting a warning, "Jimmy Jimmy Long Tail, here I come", landing seated, straddling the chain, as close to the supporting post as possible. The impetus to hurl oneself as far as possible onto the chain was always tempered by the fear of smacking into the supporting post. The intention was to get all the opposing team members seated on the chain while the members of the chain did their best not to cave in. There was little concern for the backs we landed on and how we avoided breaking any bones in that game is beyond me now!

I presume my affinity for boys' interests came about originally because of the bond I had formed with my father while I was very young. Years have tempered this, perhaps, but I am still less inclined to enjoy strictly female activities, despite the fact I am considered very feminine in nature.

No matter what the activity in those younger years, we all ran barefoot. Our sneakers were the soles of our bare feet and it pains me now to think of all the gravel roads they encountered. There was not only the gravel to contend with—there was also the problem of the black oily substance that road crews poured on the gravel to keep the dust in check. Feet had to be carefully cleaned with the garden hose before going into the house. The oily substance, I am now given to understand, contained PCBs and, statistically speaking, the carcinogenic chemicals should have done us all in long ago! Billowing clouds of dust would have followed in the wake of every passing car if the oil had not been used, and the interior of homes lining the road would have been swathed in a layer of dust. Doors and windows had to remain open during the summer months to let some air into the stiflingly hot rooms. There was no air conditioning—not even in major business establishments—and I'm not certain if electric fans existed then either. Certainly I don't recall ever seeing one during those years. In all likelihood, even if there had been fans, nobody would have been able to afford the electricity cost to operate one. Energy was conserved in every way possible, including turning off all lights in rooms that were unoccupied. I recall we often had a coal-oil lamp lit on our dining room table which was the focal point of many of the evening's activities.

We ran barefoot, and we firmly believed that dragonflies were flying sewing needles that would sew our lips together if they caught us. When we were hungry we snacked on whatever happened to be nearby. Haws were a favourite.

They were like miniature apples ranging in size from a pea to a marble. We had apples as well—green ones were the best before they had time to grow larger and ripen. There were always windfalls on the ground if one didn't feel like climbing the tree to pick them—or if we suspected the tree's owner might be looking out of the kitchen window from behind the curtains. In spring there were always the tender bottoms of some of the tall grasses to munch on, and in autumn there were hickory nuts. The nuts were so hard to crack and the meat so very difficult to pry out of the tiny, tightly packed crevices, but the wonderful taste of the nuts was more than ample reward for the effort.

During those grade school years I gradually became involved in more and more organized activities outside my home. First of all, I was enrolled in Brownies. I enjoyed working for badges—or rather I liked having new ones sewn on my uniform. I enjoyed wearing a uniform. From Brownies we graduated to Girl Guides and to more elaborate activities. We went to a camp at Colchester Beach for a week one summer. I really enjoyed the freedom of outdoor living and I even enjoyed our regimented assigned chores. My parents had never given me any real household responsibilities at home. It was a new experience for me to be entrusted with some responsibility along with the teamwork necessary to complete the assigned tasks. Also, there was the opportunity to work for more badges—special ones like building a fire without matches—that could only be achieved in the outdoor setting.

Singing around a campfire and toasting marshmallows was always a highlight of our activities. Several of the other girls and I started singing in a little group after we returned home. One of the girls, Olive, was able to sing harmony. We began to be called upon to sing at neighbourhood functions. I recall one event was held by the newly established local Horticultural Society.

On Sundays I attended a Sunday school run by the Salvation Army. Like most other neighbourhood activities, it too was held in the grade one schoolroom. One particular Sunday morning has left an indelible memory. I know I was wearing a new pale green hat my mother had crocheted for me. It had a wire in the brim that gave it shape, and it had matching grosgrain ribbons that hung down my back. The hat was in keeping with the tradition then of head coverings, gloves and Sunday-best attire for Church attendance—even bare arms were most often frowned upon.

As I crossed the wheat field, feeling quite smart in my new attire, I heard several small aircraft passing overhead—most probably destined for Walker Airport. I stopped in my tracks and watched them. I was more than a little apprehensive because I had just been hearing the news blaring from our radio at home. There had been commentaries and speeches, including one by Winston Churchill—all to do with the Battle of Britain. Now, having just minutes before heard the incessant droning of planes and the description of the havoc they wreaked, I wasn't exactly certain it was safe to walk under a flying airplane!

Sunday school was held in a little room off the main classroom—perhaps it served as a cloakroom for the grade one students. Memory fails me. However, I do remember that in that little room the Sunday school teacher made use of a sandbox with little plastic figures depicting Old Testament characters. Mirrors nestled in the sand served as lakes, and little plastic palm trees studded the sandy landscape. I use the word plastic to describe the composition of the figures. However, this was a time before plastic.

I knew many of the stories because of a book my mother had once bought for me from a door-to-door salesman. It was a children's book of Bible stories—Old Testament stories. They served as my first and only introduction to religion and to God in whom I believed most fervently, presumably through reading the fascinating stories in my book. It was a wonderful experience to see those familiar Bible stories come to life there in the sandbox.

Eventually, grade school came to an end and entrance exams were over. It was time to move on to high school. Some of us passed on the merit of our year's work. Others, who had to write the actual tests, had to travel to Edith Cavell School some distance away in order to do so. High school for the students in our community meant attending a small two-room school for grades nine and ten before entering any of the larger city high schools. Otherwise, there was a special tax that would apply—and any tax, regardless of how little, was prohibitive in those post-depression days.

The school I was destined to attend was, I believe, something like four miles from my home. That meant having to cycle there and back as there was no other means of transportation. Fortunately for me, there were no steep inclines en route because bikes in those days weren't equipped with varying speeds. One pedalled hard, and a hill meant having to pedal even harder. Being dependent upon a bicycle for my daily transportation to and from school also meant having to learn how to maintain one. Flats were commonplace so being able to fix them was paramount. My father taught me how to patch inner tubes and I can still remember the smell of the glue used to stick a patch in place. The lid of the repair kit was designed to act as a file to roughen up the smooth surface of the tube in order that the adhesive could do its job properly. I also had to learn to repair and replace uncooperative greasy bicycle chains. These had a tendency to break or come off the cogs—and broken spokes presented yet another problem. A small leather kit buckled on to the back of the bicycle seat contained all the necessary tools and was a "must" for every bike rider.

This was a time before mothers doubled as chauffeurs. In fact, most mothers couldn't drive. In any case, even if a woman could drive, there wouldn't be a car at her disposal. Families fortunate enough to have a car had only one and it would have been driven to work by the breadwinner of the family—the father. My father had gone into the plumbing business by this time so we had a truck instead of a car. It was only around this time that cars began to show signs of modernization. Until then, one had to crank a car to start up an engine, and most automobiles featured running boards—a shelf-like strip that ran beneath the doors on either side of the car to enable one to step up and into the car. I still bear the scar of a mishap when my foot slipped off a running board opening my shin to the bone. One didn't seek medical attention for such injuries in those days. We weren't familiar with tetanus shots or antibiotics, and stitches were something one had following major surgery. Our first car that I recall was a "Rochne"—a two-seater with a rumble seat. There was a small step built onto the rear fender that enabled one to step up to climb into the rumble seat. That was where I sat on any of our family outings and my mother occupied the passenger seat inside the car. Of course, there were no seat belts and I could so easily have been thrown from the car had we encountered any problem. A car horn was a small button located in the centre of the spoked steering wheel and made a distinctive "ah-ooh-ooh-gah" sound.

Women had to give up their jobs when they became pregnant. Those were the days when a girl hid her engagement ring if she really needed to find a job. An engagement meant an impending marriage and a marriage automatically meant children. Employers favoured the single girls who appeared most likely to remain on the job for a substantial period of time. Once a girl started a family, her career became that of housewife and mother—a homemaker. There were only rare exceptions to the rule and one I can recall was "The Shoe Lady"—a woman who ran a small shoe repair shop that housed a very talkative parrot in addition to an assortment of smells of leather and polish. A woman also ran the local post office. There was a woman who gave piano lessons for a modest cost, and another who made several kinds of fudge that she sold door-to-door. There was also a beauty shop set in the home of one of the neighbourhood women. I went to her shop once with my girlfriend Annie who was getting a permanent. My nostrils still quiver at the memory of the pungent chemicals used to turn her straight hair into rivulets of tiny waves that could be set into curls

Jobs in those days were for men in order that they could support their families. That's the way it was. Paid maternity leave and day-care were not only unheard of in those days, they were unimaginable!

CHAPTER 5

❀

My first day of high school marked several milestones in my life. It marked the day of my first period—my official entry into womanhood. It also marked the day a very special boy named Victor caught my eye. Victor was a tall, slender boy with wide shoulders and an equally wide smile. I found his curly auburn hair and bright blue eyes as beguiling as his friendly manner. For the first time in my life I no longer wanted a boy simply as a friend. I was in love! I was sure I was in love because I had never felt that way about a boy before, and it came as no surprise when I discovered that Victor felt the same way about me. It all seemed perfectly natural.

I knew about women's periods—other girls had told me. I also knew how babies were made—other girls had told me that, as well. I remember thinking, just as most young people do, that there must surely be some exceptions because most assuredly my parents never did anything like that! There were no articles anywhere that one could read. The whole subject was universally taboo. Ignorance prevailed giving much room for old wives' tales to run rampant—and all in hushed whispers, of course.

I noticed that my mother had begun inspecting my underwear each night after I had gone to bed. At last I realized why when one morning she placed all the necessities—a sanitary belt, a folded cloth and safety pins on my bed. She said, "You'll have to start wearing these now," and walked out of the room with no explanation. I knew what to do but thought she might have more to tell me. Surely there were things I needed to know? And why did my mother assume I knew anything at all when we had never ever discussed the subject! One thing I did know. It suddenly dawned on me when I picked up the folded cloth. From time to time throughout the years I had noticed large squares of freshly laundered cloth being bleached by the sun on the patch of grass behind our house. It had never occurred to me to wonder about their purpose. I don't know whether commercial sanitary napkins were even available or not anywhere—in a drug store perhaps. If pads were available, I wonder how many would have had the nerve to ask for them. The concept of Tampons was most certainly a thing of the future.

That evening as my mother sat out on the front steps, I went out and sat beside her. It was growing dark and I felt that would make things less embarrassing. Her response to my questioning was simply, "You have to have monthlies so you can have babies." This statement came as quite a shock to me because, up to that point, I hadn't made any connection between the various bits of information I had learned. I had once seen a woman in an advanced state of pregnancy but hadn't pondered on how the baby had managed to develop within her or how it would eventually exit from her. Perhaps the sight of her huge belly had embarrassed me sufficiently that I had tried to erase any further thought of it. In those days, when a woman began "showing", she was expected to go into seclusion and make every attempt to keep her altered state as inconspicuous as possible.

When I couldn't pry any further information from my mother regarding my new status in life, I purposely said something which I had absolutely no intention of doing. I said, "Then I'll ask Dad." "Men don't know anything about these things," was my mother's instant response and I detected the note of near alarm in her voice as she said it. At that point I believed her. So ended my lesson on the subject of becoming a woman.

My school lessons were a different story. We were two grades, nine and ten, housed in a two-room building. As a result, each class remained throughout the day in its own room and with an established seating arrangement. This gave us more time, I believe, for our studies. We enjoyed art and music, as well as music appreciation classes, in addition to the necessary science, maths, English, social studies and phys ed. Physical education was a required subject in those days but, without a gymnasium, our activities were limited to those that could be conducted outdoors. Our music teacher formed our class into a choir and we were eventually chosen to sing several songs at a Teacher's Convention. I was singing alto parts at that time.

Whether by accident or by design, Victor's desk was located right behind mine. We soon began exchanging notes throughout the day—notes that told of our innermost thoughts, our hopes and dreams, and all that we aspired to do as grownups.

On warm evenings I would sit out on our front steps doing my homework as I watched for Victor to ride by on his bicycle. He lived a few miles away so the trip by my house was purposely orchestrated. We would wave discreetly, sharing our secret pleasure. Several times just at dusk, when I thought I wouldn't be detected, I had the courage to slip out onto the street to meet him. I would perch on the bar of his bike and we would ride around the block occasionally stealing a kiss while our hearts beat wildly. Unlike today life moved slowly and dating was still some time away. I was, however, allowed to attend Victor's birthday party one Saturday night in October during our second year of high school. I floated on cloud nine—I was actually in his living room—I was actually speaking with his parents! When we played the game of spin the bottle and I got to accompany Victor to the other room for a kiss, I thought my heart would burst with happiness as he held me tightly and whispered, "Just think—right here in my own house." I knew then what a special moment it was for him too.

When we had finished our two years at the township high school, Victor and I both elected to go to the vocational school in town. Victor enrolled in a technical course while I entered a commercial program.

As soon as I had begun classes in the city I discovered gym. I had never been to a school that housed a gymnasium. A whole new world opened before me! Although I loved the vaults on the horse, the balance beam was my special favourite and soon became my forte. My gym teacher went out of her way to tell me how proud she was of my progress. I had entered her classes timidly and stiffly aware of my body as I made my self-conscious attempts in front of the others—feeling that every eye in the room was upon me. But I soon lost myself to the enjoyment of the movement. I began to relax and, of course, I began to adapt easily and naturally. My teacher said that it had been very gratifying to watch me come out of my shell. Very soon I became a member of the gymnastic team and spent many enjoyable hours under the guidance of the sympathetic teacher whose few words of encouragement had inspired and propelled me to excel.

There were also other aspects of my high school years that opened up a whole new world to me. Calls went out for students to try out for parts in a play. They were casting *Little Women*. At one time I would never have dared try out but, somehow, someone persuaded me to read. I don't remember how it came about nor do I recall feeling especially nervous as I sat waiting my turn to read. When the time came I just read the lines as I saw them and before I knew it I had been cast as Meg, the eldest sister. What fun! I'm not certain now whether my mother made my costumes or whether they were rented from Malabar's. I am inclined to think they were rented because the elaborate hoop skirts would have meant a great deal of work. In any case, I felt absolutely wonderful in my pale blue satin gown with my long dark hair done up in a bouffant and make-up on my face. It was the first time I had ever seen myself made up. I rather liked what I saw in the mirror, apart from the red dots at the corners of my eyes. Those, I was told, made my eyes appear either larger or set further apart—I've forgotten which. But, in either case, I would think the dots were unnecessary because my eyes are both large and wide-set and appeared to be even more so in those youthful years.

Tea Dances were one of the highlights of our high school years. The dances were held in the gymnasium at regular intervals. They were held immediately after classes so there was sufficient opportunity to be home by suppertime. That's the only reason I was able to attend. My parents didn't approve of dancing and oh, how I loved to dance! I neglected to inform them when I arrived home that it had been a dance that had detained me. There were so many legitimate after-school clubs and activities that my late arrival home was nothing out of the ordinary. Fortunately, my father was unable to check on my movements once I started school in the city. He had often chastised me for my supposed "conduct" while attending the township school. I can only assume that my father made enquiries because I don't believe I ever did anything out of the ordinary that would have prompted other children to tattle. I was simply doing my best to integrate with my peers. Looking back, it was indeed an age of innocence and through my naivety I was perhaps the most innocent of all! Nevertheless, it seemed I was always guilty of something.

In those days a girl dated a number of boys—even if she felt attracted to one in particular. It was an accepted rule that there was safety in numbers. "Going steady" meant that a couple had crossed the line into something more than a perfunctory goodnight kiss and had developed a serious relationship that would ultimately lead to marriage. Dating one person seriously implied some measure of intimacy—and intimacy was not an accepted part of the dating scene in those days. It was all very different from today's mindset.

Despite the social dictates and customs of the time, however, my parents continued to march to their own drum—with principles even more rigid than those of an already moral society that they believed was moderating too quickly. They were attempting to raise a daughter with the constraints by which they had been raised with no allowance for the fact that time and circumstance had altered during forty-some years.

I was not allowed to date and this led to embarrassment on occasion. One Christmas holiday a boy who had been trying to persuade me to go out with him arrived at our front door with a gift in hand. My father met him at the door and informed him, in no uncertain terms, that I was not accepting gifts. The talk was all over the school when we returned to classes at the end of the holiday. I was mortified!

I made a new friend when I began City School—Fran. I'm not certain what led us to become friends because we had as much similarity as chalk and cheese. Fran and I were as unlike as two girls could be and yet we quickly became inseparable. She was shorter than I and smaller boned. Her clear blue eyes were set in a heart-shaped face framed by blonde wavy hair. I felt I towered over Fran, and my smokey dark eyes and hair were in vivid contrast to her fairness. I envied Fran for the sense of self-assurance she seemed to possess. This, I surmised, came from having steadfast beliefs and a sense of belonging—both of which seemed to emanate from her religious background. Fran had attended a Catholic school for her primary education and was a devout Catholic. Through Fran I began to attend Catholic students meetings held after classes each week.

To say that my parents would not approve of my attending the meetings would be a gross understatement. I discerned early on that my mother considered Catholics to be ritualistic pagans who "bought" their way into Heaven. I had gleaned this information from her in answer to my questions the day we attended a Catholic Mass when our butcher passed away. As a young child I was taken to view many corpses and attend many funerals. I don't believe that parents today subject their children to these realities unless the deceased is a close friend or immediate family.

Victor was Roman Catholic, as was my new best friend, Fran. I needed to know more about the faith that guided the people I had befriended and loved. One of the things I learned quite early in the lessons was that dancing was not a sin. Now this was a religion I could agree with! The way it was explained was that it was one's approach to the dance that mattered. Dancing too closely or allowing an improper thought—that's where the element of sin arose. As far as I was concerned, the free movement to the music was exhilarating. It was liberating—an end in itself. Any sexual connotation didn't exist in my mind and, as a result, I felt quite justified in being my own judge as to whether or not I should be dancing. I felt no remorse about keeping that part of my activities hidden from my parents. Dancing was not a sin and that was all the confirmation I needed. However, I didn't go so far as to enquire about my keeping the activity secret from my parents. If that was wrong then I didn't want to know about it!

My English teacher was another person who had a profound effect in bolstering my self-esteem during those high school days. I soon discovered I enjoyed every conceivable aspect of her English course and, not only that, I was a born public speaker! I made it into the finals in the public speaking contest and had the opportunity of addressing an assembly of the entire school. Unfortunately, the subject I drew for my impromptu speech was so similar in nature to my prepared presentation, I could think of little else to say except to reiterate what I had already said.

At the end of my graduating year my English teacher took me aside to explain she was giving me an overall mark of ninety-nine, although my actual mark had been one hundred. She explained that the deduction was deliberate on her part since no one could be "perfect" in English. She also encouraged me to consider borrowing from the Alumni Fund and go on to University to pursue a career in Journalism. I was thrilled at the prospect! Imagine carrying on studying and doing something one loved. It wouldn't seem like working; it would be having fun and eventually getting paid for it. Until that moment I had assumed I would carry on with the stenographic career my father had chosen for me. My mother had seen me as a commercial artist. I had often seen myself as a teacher or someone in the medical profession—perhaps a nurse.

Commercial courses also included several classes in Home Economics each week in order to round out our education. I was interested in cooking and in sewing but somehow these classes managed to spell disaster for me. I spent a good many of them sitting out in the hall—the punishment at that time for errant students. Try as I might, I seemed totally unable to get in synch with the Home Economics teacher. She made short work of my reputation as a "model" student. Fortunately, the Vice-Principal, saw me in a different light and seemed quite amused at finding me out in the hall so frequently. His attitude gave me the impression that circumstance played some part in the matter and that I wasn't really the failure I was beginning to suspect I might be.

Actually, my Home Economics teacher and I ended up on the best of terms. She was staging a fashion show for some charity—it may have been the Red Cross—and she selected me as one of the models. The show was held somewhere outside the school. I think it was in one of the downtown department stores of the day, Smith's or Bartlett, McDonald and Gow. I do recall her saying that I was a perfect size. That statement certainly came as music to the ears of someone who saw in the mirror that certain parts of her anatomy appeared to be much too small while another part seemed much too large!

Thinking back, the show may have been staged at Smith's. Our school seemed to have a liaison with that store. Each year we took it over *en masse* for a day and sales clerks were replaced with senior students. As our compensation, at lunchtime we were treated to fare at the Norton Palmer Hotel. I had my picture in the Star "selling" some toiletries to the Principal of our school. I remember it was Coty Emeraude. I'm not even certain that scent still exists.

In our graduating year we gained a lot of hands-on experience. Each of the commercial students had their day manning the school switchboard—an old fashioned board with plug-in wires. I can't help but smile each time I see pictures of Lily Tomlin portraying Ernestine, the telephone operator, seated at one of those consoles. We were also each assigned as secretary to one of the teachers. I was secretary to the Foundry teacher—a jovial Scotsman who had a penchant for baking scones in the foundry furnace when classes were out. It was a delight to work for him.

During our final summer holiday before graduation, we were all obliged to work at the Ford Motor Company in whatever capacity we were being trained. The boys from the technical courses, who studied subjects like auto mechanics, foundry and machine shop, were naturally assigned to different areas of the factory. Those of us who were from the commercial courses were assigned to office routines. My job was to type "supply mechs". These were lists of auto parts typed on legal sized stencils for the purpose of mimeographing. It was before Xerox machines. Duplication required stencils—sheets of film that one perforated with the typewriter keys. After they had been typed, the stencils were then spread out on an ink bed and the printing transferred by running blank sheets of paper across the stencils. Multiple copies were obtained by feeding the paper by means of a crank. More modern versions of the contraption were motorized.

We were paid a modest wage for our efforts that summer, and our money was direct deposited to an account set up for each of us at a nearby bank. With my very first salary I bought a pair of luggage tan leather shoes with high heels and matching leather handbag. All things were relative in those days. If I recall correctly, that first paycheque was somewhere in the thirty-dollar neighbourhood and, after the shoes and bag, I still had money left to pay for my transportation and other expenses.

CHAPTER 6

❀

My father was a very practical man and, as he had only a modest income, he wouldn't hear of my English teacher's suggestion of borrowing alumni funds to attend University. His reasoning was that once I had graduated I would marry instead of going on to earn an income to repay the loan. At that time his rationale seemed plausible, because it seemed to be the ambition of most girls to eventually be married—which meant giving up their jobs and staying home once the babies began to arrive. Whatever circumstance might provide by way of my being able to repay the loan could only be speculated, of course. There was little else to do but apply for a job in the field for which I had been trained.

And so it was. I was hired as a cashier-stenographer in a small branch of an insurance company. It was a job. I had an income. I was unhappy. I used as much of my weekly pay as I could afford—after I had paid board money to my mother—to pursue interests that inspired me. It was usual for working children to contribute something to the household, if only to help offset the grocery bill. My mother saved the money I paid her and bought furniture for my bedroom. I began studying voice. I joined a dance studio to learn tap dancing and ballet. I joined a health club. I joined a boys and girls brass band and learned to play an E-flat bass—learning to play well enough to march in parades. I loved my band uniform. It consisted of a bright red blazer with a white skirt for the girls—boys wore white trousers—and we each wore a black officers' hat with a smart gold crest above the visor. My after-work activities helped make up for the sheer boredom of my daily routine. I had no idea who I was or what I wanted. I was searching for I knew not what and, despite the fact I had friends, I was very lonely.

The Second World War was in full swing. Boys across the country had been enlisting as soon as they reached the defining age of eighteen, and many local young men had joined them at "the front". By the time we completed high school, Victor had become old enough to join the Air Force. This was his long-cherished dream and one he had shared with me in one of the many notes that had passed between us during our days at our former high school. The only thing different was that his dream was to be a pilot—instead he became an air-gunner. Victor apparently lacked the necessary mathematical skills to become a pilot.

Victor was dating other girls but I was still not allowed to date. However, on his last night in the city before leaving for training camp in Quebec, Victor asked if I would be able to go with him to the farewell party he and some of his squadron had arranged. It was to be a house party—just a small gathering. Wonder of wonders, I was allowed to go! It was my first real date. And I remember exactly every detail of what I wore. I even wore the luggage tan shoes I had acquired with my first paycheque from Ford's.

There must have been drinking at the party—I don't honestly recall. Alcohol wasn't such a big deal with young people then. There was music, of course, provided by a record player and a stack of 78s, and we danced. I don't recall how Victor and I ended up in an adjoining bedroom—on a bed amidst a heap of coats. Victor kissed me and held me close to him—much closer than I had ever been held. At one point he touched my breast. I had never been touched in intimate places before and I could feel myself tense in response. Uncertain as to whether I liked it or not, I was filled with a tumult of conflicting emotions. Victor sensed my hesitancy and made no attempt to take things any further. He knew the future was ours and that we didn't need to rush headlong into anything. When the party ended and we said goodnight, Victor asked if I'd accompany him to the train station next morning to see him off. Of course I would!

My friend Annie and I had witnessed many of the Sunday evening departures of troop trains filled with enlisted men who were bound for overseas. We were drawn by the magnetism of the real life drama—the tears and emotional farewells, the band that played as the train slowly departed, and servicemen hanging from the train windows for a last look at loved ones left standing on the station platform. Those who were left behind stood forlornly, awash in tears, not knowing whether one day they might see "his" picture in the daily newspaper along with all the others who were listed as killed or missing in action.

But on the Sunday morning when I went to the same station to say farewell to my love, there was no crowd, no band, no tearful farewell—only his parents and me. Victor wasn't leaving for overseas. He was going to Valleyfield, Quebec, for commando training, and would be returning home for an embarkation leave at its completion. We would cross the next bridge when we came to it.

Little did we realize while waiting for the train that beautiful, sunny autumn Sunday morning that, at the end of his training, Victor would be shipped directly overseas—without his much anticipated leave.

Letters soon began arriving, and sometimes a photo as well. I wrote to Victor regularly. Occasionally I was able to send a parcel to him—chocolate bars, chewing gum, and toiletries. All the little things we once took for granted and that had now become so difficult to obtain. It would take a while before I could collect enough goodies to make up a worthwhile parcel to send. Many of the items were rationed and our ration cards, allowing each citizen their fair share, were quite limiting. Not only were the rations strict, there was also the problem of availability. Substitution and inventiveness were the keywords during those days when most everything was in short supply. One required a ration card for sugar and ration tokens for meat and any of its bi-products. There was a good deal of recycling as well—quite different from our environmental efforts of the present day. One item in particular, I recall, was leftover fat and grease from cooking. This was required for the making of soap which was in extremely short supply. It seemed that everyone used bluing to colour their homemade soap. I picture tubs of the mushy stuff whenever I see a modern-day bar of blue soap.

Victor's letters to me were usually about England and the people whom he met. He managed to convey something of his new environment despite the censorship of the day. It was nothing for a paragraph or two to be blacked out by a censor's markings. Censorship was very strict—almost ruthless at times—but it was a necessity. No communication of any kind could be allowed to reveal even the slightest bit of information that would be useful to the enemy. What we might consider an offhand comment could, indeed, perhaps spell disaster in those serious times. One motto of the day was, "Loose lips sink ships."

I, in turn, wrote to Victor about my new job and all the after-work activities I was engaged in. By this time I had begun going to dances twice a week—Thursdays and Saturdays at Coral Gables. I went with my friend Fran and between us we had a circle of friends with whom we danced each evening.

A live orchestra with featured vocalists provided the music. In winter, the dances were held in a large upstairs hall downtown. In summer they were held upstairs behind the grandstand at Jackson Park. That was closer to my home and I was able to walk there and home afterward. Going home meant crossing a large vacant field, and then following a path beside the tracks for a short way in order to reach the street that led to our neighbourhood. I can still recall all the night sounds—the chirping of the crickets and the incessant croaking of the frogs in the marshy area along the tracks. Those were the days and nights long before there was any fear of walking alone at night—anywhere. One walked alone without fear and doors were left unlocked. There was no reason for people to barricade themselves or to walk with caution. It was an age of innocence—a simple life, uncomplicated by violent crimes and predators.

When Victor and I had finally exhausted news of our new circumstances, we began to talk of things we would do when he arrived back home. He had never had the opportunity to attend the dances and I was looking forward to the first time we could go dancing together. Victor had learned to drive a car and talked eagerly of borrowing his father's car.

Victor's father died while he was overseas and Victor was not allowed compassionate leave to come home for the funeral. I attended, along with a couple of our former classmates, and felt in a small way that I was joined with Victor in his grief.

I have absolutely no recollection of how I came to know that the unthinkable had happened. Victor's plane was shot down over Germany on one of his last scheduled missions! I was stunned! In shock might be a more apt description. I felt numb. With the confident assurance of the young that death could never touch them, Victor and I had never discussed that possibility. I hadn't feared for him. I missed him while he was away and our letters spoke only of the future. Perhaps it was through one of my letters being returned, or perhaps it was through a notice in the newspaper that I came to know the tragic news. In any event, I was ill prepared to cope. I held my grief inside as I went woodenly about my daily routine.

One evening I overheard my father speaking downstairs. He was relating the news of Victor's death to someone and, after my initial surprise that my father knew such details, something within me gave way at the sound of the words being spoken aloud. My pent-up tears flowed for hours

In the morning my eyes were puffy beyond recognition but the tears had done nothing to lessen my grief for the boy who lay buried in Duisdorf cemetery, three miles southwest of Bonn, Germany. Strangely enough, after all these many years—marriage, children, and other loves—Victor still enters my dreams on occasion

Life went on after that, just as it always does. I continued to go through the motions of daily life. I continued to go to the office. I went to my ballet classes. I continued on with my voice lessons as well, and my teacher noticed a marked change in my range. I could no longer manage the bright and lilting soprano repertoire I had been studying. My voice was now more suited to songs of a mezzo-soprano's range, soul stirring and mournful.

I was drifting—simply existing. I felt I had nowhere to turn nor did I want to. I felt totally devoid of emotion and without any incentive to carry on. I shared my feelings with no one. Withdrawal was second nature to me. I have no idea what perception my friends and acquaintances had of me during this period, and certainly none gave any indication—at least none that I noticed.

This was the situation when an acquaintance suggested I accept a date with the man his uncle worked for. The man's name was Jack and he had expressed a desire to meet me after seeing my photograph in the newspaper. Having one's photo in the local paper wasn't an uncommon occurrence in our fairly small community. I was told that Jack was single, and handsome as well, but I think it was more the desperate need for a glimmer of light in my life—some diversion—that prompted me to accept. I don't believe I was in any frame of mind to be thinking clearly about anything, much less giving any thought to finding a new love.

Jack was older and even more handsome than his description had led me to believe. He was tall and well built, with blonde hair and grey-green eyes, and his jovial nature was very appealing. Jack owned his own business and could afford to take me on outings and to the types of restaurants which boys my own age would be unable to do. Jack had an air of authority and accomplishment about him that instilled in me a sense of security and well being. His take-charge attitude left little room for me to be concerned with any serious thought of where my life might be headed. I was simply enjoying the luxury of being cared for.

At the time he had asked for the introduction, Jack had placed a large sum of money in our friend's bank account to verify he had sufficient means to apply for residency in the United States. Naively, I saw this as a most generous gesture and, furthermore, I was flattered by the attention Jack paid me—attention I so desperately needed!

It was not difficult for me to become infatuated and quickly become serious about Jack, not realizing for one moment what a profound effect meeting him would have on my life!

CHAPTER 7

❁

With my photographs all packed, I couldn't help but think how many more there would have been had I not deliberately destroyed them. Destroying photographs, I've learned, does not eradicate the image already embedded in the mind's eye. I could still see them all so clearly—but dare not let myself dwell on them.

From my earliest childhood it had always been my fervent desire to "grow up and have babies"—six boys and all with red hair as I had often told my mother. This was long before I ever met the auburn-haired Victor. Yet, when confronted with the realization that I was pregnant, my first reaction was one of total disbelief. As had been my pattern in life, I held the information to myself—one moment in a state of panic not knowing what to do and the next not believing it to be true. I lived with denial until the day my mother confronted me.

It was only after my mother berated me for not having the sense to get married that I finally acknowledged my secret. My mother's stern warning was that under no circumstance was my father to know of the pregnancy. The situation at home offered no solution to my dilemma. It weighed heavily on my mind to the point where my inattentiveness at the office gave rise to my dismissal. How now to keep things secret?

I finally confided in my best friend, Fran, who seemed mostly concerned that her mother might find out. By this time I believe my situation was beginning to become obvious. Fran had no more idea than I when it came to formulating a solution. I knew I must keep the baby—of this I was certain. At that point it was the only thing of which I was certain. Despite the fact that society shunned unwed mothers, and despite the risks of financial hardship, I refused to accept the impracticality of a girl still in her teens raising a child alone without either emotional or financial support.

Eventually, the pianist and the ballet teacher at the dance studio I was still attending recognized my symptoms and—without words—gave me the support I so sorely needed. Yvonne, my ballet teacher, realized that I would have to leave my parents' house. She invited me to stay with her family until I was able to formulate concrete plans.

In the first few weeks I stayed at Yvonne's, I was encouraged to have a medical check-up, and she kindly arranged this with her own doctor. She also encouraged me to have another talk with Jack, the baby's father.

I will never forget the night I went to speak with Jack. He had not returned my several phone calls, so I took the initiative of going to his office. It was a snowy night and I was not familiar with the neighbourhood. I walked for blocks—possibly more than a mile—and arrived at his office building looking somewhat like a snowman. I stood on the sidewalk and saw him sitting with some other people in a front office at street level. He glanced up and saw me. A moment later he came out to where I stood. Jack led me to his car and proceeded to drive me back to some transportation. I've forgotten all of our conversation, except for his words, "I'll have fifty witnesses to swear I've never laid eyes on you." Those words ring in my ears to this day. It was more than obvious that the attentive man who had filled me with such a sense of well being was, in reality, not someone I could count on in this time of crisis. Jack lived close by, as far as distance is concerned. However, an international border stretched between us and Jack relied heavily upon this protection.

Actually, it turned out to be a wake-up call for both of us. While I was absorbing the fact that I was on my own, and that Jack had not been serious about our relationship, he was hit with the news that our mutual friend had cleared out the bank account containing the loan monies and had disappeared!

I made arrangements then to leave Yvonne and her family. I packed up and went to another city where I approached the Salvation Army. They had a fine reputation for coming to the aid of pregnant girls.

In those days, girls who found themselves in my difficult situation either went to a Salvation Army home for unwed mothers or, if they had compassionate families, were sent "to visit an aunt" for a while. This coded language meant one of two things: either arrangements had been made for them to travel to another city where they could stay undetected at a Salvation Army home—giving up their babies before returning—or an illegal abortion had been arranged somewhere and they could return following their recuperation.

In either case, they could eventually return home with their good reputations still intact.

The Salvation Army enabled me to be placed in a good home where I could work for my room and board. I was fortunate enough to find myself in a happy home belonging to a family of four that included a four-year old boy and a baby girl. The family lived in an affluent section of the city and, indeed, their home was beautifully decorated and furnished. I had never lived in such sumptuous surroundings and I took a good deal of pleasure in my light housework duties. Dusting never felt like a chore.

The head of the household, Mr. Patterson, was a noted lawyer and Mrs. Patterson's family boasted the inclusion of a famous Hollywood actor. Mr. Patterson's brother was a leading surgeon in that city. In all, their circle of friends was extensive and they entertained quite frequently. It was such a treat to be included in all the lavish preparations and I learned to prepare and appreciate some very interesting dishes during my time with them. To my delight, I found I had an innate interest in cooking and this opened up a whole new world to me—one that holds my interest to this day. Even more important to me at the time, however, was the warmth and genuine caring the family and their friends showered upon me. I was never alone in the kitchen for long. There was always someone popping in to enquire how I was feeling or to praise me for something I had managed to concoct—and to spend a few minutes just chatting. Dr. Patterson, in particular, was a tease. He would always come to check the progress of "the watermelon seed I had swallowed."

It was during my stay at the Patterson's that I also learned about fashion. Until then, my only regard for clothes had been something that should simply fit well and look good. It was with great interest that I watched Mrs. Patterson undergo a transformation to Dior's "New Look" which had become the current fashion trend. Her clothes were all classic in line and obviously expensive. Rather than making a lot of new purchases, she would let a hem down here, make a few alterations there, and buy a new skirt to go with an existing jacket, or change her accessories. Lo and behold, a whole new beautiful wardrobe would appear with very little effort or expenditure. I was enthralled! I had discovered yet another latent talent that I began to develop. A love of fine fabrics and creating original garments have been part of my life ever since. It was during that period at the Patterson home that I began to realize there was an artistic side of me that was far stronger than I had been aware. In later years I was fortunate enough to take an evening course under the tutorship of a former

Paris design house worker and learned pattern making from individual measurements.

The knowledge I gained in the Patterson home, and the warmth with which the family members and their guests treated me, were the only silver lining in one of the darkest clouds of my life. Much as I longed for children of my own, the prospect was bittersweet indeed under the circumstances.

When the time came for me to give birth, I went from the warmth of the Patterson family setting to the hospital. Although I was treated with kindness and had excellent care, I was frightened and alone in the cold, sterile surroundings—and ignorant of what to expect. I had not anticipated such pain when giving birth and was totally unprepared for the experience. But finally, I held my son in my arms and that was all that mattered to me at that moment

My friend Fran and her fiancé Bob came to visit me in hospital, and so did Mrs. Patterson and one of her many friends whom I had met previously. Everyone was generous in their praise of my son and this was not unexpected because he was a beautiful baby. Their gifts and good wishes touched me—especially the fact that Fran and Bob had travelled a long distance to visit us for those few moments.

Looking back, I wonder that no one made an effort to dissuade me from keeping my baby. Was I so adamant in my determination to keep him? Did I appear, as was noted in a social worker's profile of me, to have above average intelligence that seemingly afforded me the ability to make a rational decision? Whether my decision was the right one or not, it was nevertheless my decision—and one I did my very best to live with.

I named my baby after his father and, in the belief that Jack's name had been a derivative of John, that is the name I used for the birth registration. My father's name was Albert, so my son was named John Albert.

My parents had moved to a cottage area on the shores of Lake Huron during the months of our separation, undoubtedly to escape the curiosity of prying neighbours. My father had recently retired so they were free to move as they pleased. That's where my son and I went, at my parents' invitation, when we finally left the hospital.

The magic of a baby, of course, erased any negative feelings my father had toward my situation. He doted on his grandson! We didn't discuss how long John and I would stay and I was in no hurry to do so at that time. Clearly I needed an income before I could do anything on my own and, meanwhile, knowing John would be well cared for was one less thing I had to worry about.

I tended to my baby's needs and helped my mother with some of the housework and then, for a part of the day, I worked as a cashier at a small convenience store just a block away from my parents' cottage. The meagre salary I made at the store wasn't nearly enough to provide for our needs so I combed the classified section of the daily newspaper hoping to find something more lucrative.

At last I saw an ad for someone to write commercial copy for the local radio station. I wrote a letter explaining that, although I had no actual experience, I did feel qualified. Obviously someone agreed with me on the strength of the letter I wrote and, following an interview, I was hired. In addition to my job as continuity writer, I was eventually given some on-air experience in the form of a talk show. It was a late afternoon show of interest to commuters on the road home. Little John was my biggest fan.

I loved the work at the radio station. I was much more suited to it than to the secretarial work I had been trained for. I soon became heavily involved in radio drama as well and, through those connections, landed the lead in a local theatre group's production of *Joan of Lorraine*. Unfortunately, a New York actress who had previously played the role of Joan had to be called to do the actual production. I chose that particular time to be extremely ill with mumps, of all things!

With some assistance from my parents, we managed to struggle through several years together—emotionally difficult years, although little John was never the source of the problem.

John was a happy boy—inquisitive, smiling and most loving. I clung to the hope that his father would love us both sufficiently to marry us. I had contacted John's father to let him know that he had a son and he appeared quite eager to make the long-distance drive as often as possible in order to visit us. His interest in the baby seemed genuine and I began to believe that he perhaps loved me as well. Most certainly I thought I loved him, despite his rejection at the news of my pregnancy.

It's so ironic that the contempt society held for unwed mothers in those days should be shared by the very one who had been a party to the cause. Perhaps somewhere in the back of my mind I could understand Jack's reluctance to be a part of my predicament while I was pregnant. Given the public moral sentiment of the day, perhaps I even shared that opinion of myself. In any event, the resurgence of Jack's interest in me once the baby had been born caused me to hope against hope. In hindsight I realize how naïve I was to think that physical closeness equated genuine caring.

I lived a strange existence—not daring to let my new colleagues and acquaintances know of my circumstance for fear of their rejection, while at the same time my personal life revolved around the son I adored. I was so proud of him! I deplored the fact my life had to be so compartmentalized in order to function and survive; yet somehow it came very naturally to me. The training I had in maintaining my "secret age" throughout my entire childhood proved to be invaluable. I had an unrelenting feeling of pressure that had eventually become second nature to me.

My entire life, it seemed, had been one of duplicity. There was scarcely a memory of a time I had ever felt free to be myself. From my earliest recollection I had felt pressured to hide my own feelings—to be all that someone else expected me to be—never seemingly allowed to be the person I really was!

In truth, I had never been given the opportunity to learn who I was and I had long ago lost sight of my own true self.

CHAPTER 8

⚘

Modern methods of birth control were unknown in those days and, even if they had been, it wouldn't have been a suitable topic for discussion. "Nice" girls certainly wouldn't equip themselves. There were no specialized agencies to dispense advice such as exist today, and there was many a victim of old wives' tales. This is how it was at the time I was confronted by the reality that, as a result of my continued relationship with John's father, I was once again pregnant!

All over again I was caught in a whirlpool of emotions—desperation, fear, anger—but perhaps mostly heartbreak. Ironically, I had just been offered a scriptwriting job in the city where John had been born. I found it so gratifying to have been sought out for the position, and financially it was certainly a boon. I had accepted without hesitation and it was only once I'd made the move that I was faced with the realization of my pregnancy.

I had nowhere to turn. By this time I had finally wakened to the fact that Jack's interest in me would never lead to the married life I so dearly longed for. I wanted a life with emotional and financial stability. I needed to raise my children in a loving home with dignity and respect, which I now knew that Jack had no intention of ever providing. He had taken advantage of me, a love-struck teenager, lost in an emotional jungle without the guidance of her parents who were good people, but simply lacking the skills to raise an active, inquisitive, and headstrong daughter.

Many things, it seemed, my parents had just "expected" me to know—but I didn't know! There was a total lack of communication or understanding—a mind-boggling circumstance to me now, but accepted at the time as the norm. Quite simply, I had no terms of reference with which to properly compare our dismal situation. Though I was now no longer a teenager, I was still obviously totally unaware of who I was or where I was headed, and I was emotionally immature, to say the least.

At the time I began my new job I answered an ad in the paper to share a large apartment with three other girls. I thought it would be the most economical arrangement until I became established and could bring John to live with me. I had just moved in when realization of my situation dawned. Confronted with this pregnancy, I was soon forced to give up my new writing job but not before I had been faced with considerable ridicule.

Although the girls in the apartment were not happy with the state of things, they were charitable and allowed me to stay on while I endeavoured to sort things out. One of the girls, Margo, attempted to help by contacting my mother. She thought I was too ashamed to tell my mother of my situation, but felt I needed a mother's tender care. I only learned of this when my irate mother called me that evening from a pay phone so her conversation would not be overheard on the phone line they shared with several neighbours. She told me emphatically that since "I had made my bed, I must now lie in it." I asked about John as the tears came rolling down my cheeks. My mother responded that he was all right but that I could forget about seeing him until I had gotten myself out of the mess I was in. The tone of my mother's voice and the prospect of not seeing my son for months sent me into near hysterics. I slumped down onto the floor beside the phone and literally dissolved. My apartment mates quickly went from being bystanders to caregivers and comforters. Dorothy was the one I shared a room with—I've forgotten the name of the girl who shared with Margo. Regardless of names, I don't know how I could have survived without them!

When they saw I was inconsolable they summoned my doctor who was only a short distance away. They saw to it that I took the prescribed sedation and tucked me into bed. It was Margo, the one who had tried to help by calling my mother, who arranged with one of her colleagues at work to take me into his home. Tom and his wife Marion showered me with kindness and in repayment would accept no thanks. I was told to simply pass the favour along should I ever encounter someone else in need. As a young man, Tom had been helped by an old sea captain who would accept no thanks for his extreme generosity other than a promise to "pass it on". I happened to become the beneficiary of that outstanding debt—one that I have endeavoured to repay at every opportunity since those dark days of my life.

Life went on automatically during those months. I was in deep despair. I ate, I slept, and I helped Marion with household chores and cooking. I have few recollections of events—not even of how or where I spent that Christmas. The baby was due in April. Some time prior to that April date I spent a few days in hospital, as it appeared I might be in premature labour. I'm certain Fran and I must have corresponded during those months, but I have no recollection. Fran and Bob had married shortly after John was born and I had attended the wedding. I was very proud of the fact that I had introduced the two of them—Bob was my date originally. Once I had introduced the two of them, the rest was history. They were my friends and they loved me unconditionally. I felt blessed to have them in my life.

With the imminent birth of a second child, I finally admitted to myself that I could no longer cope. I was not capable of handling the demands that faced me. Quite simply, I was too young, too immature, and totally exhausted both emotionally and physically. I was shunned by society and too thin-skinned to handle it. An unwed mother in those days was a social outcast, although there were those generous souls who could ultimately forgive a girl for her mistake, if she appeared to be of good moral fibre and genuinely contrite—after all, everyone makes a mistake at some time or other. A second pregnancy to an unwed girl was totally unacceptable—the girl was obviously incorrigible!

Society did not acknowledge unwed mothers, so neither did society provide assistance programs for them. Organizations were in place to help girls give up their babies—but none to assist in keeping them.

There was even less likelihood now of my ever marrying or of being able to provide a good home for my children. Men were reluctant to openly date single girls with children—those who did were not interested in a serious relationship. Such girls were, for the most part, considered "fair game"—easy targets. In many cases their loneliness and lack of self-esteem bore out this unkind notion. Certainly there were exceptions but, for the most part, men behaved in a manner that they felt most acceptable to the majority.

"Conformity" rather than "individuality" was the code of the day. To date an unwed mother openly in a serious relationship would in no way conform and would only serve to bring society's judgment down upon the man himself. My reputation was damaged beyond repair.

I was finally faced with the reality that if there was to be a future for any of us, I would have to give up the new baby for adoption. John, too, deserved a home and a family life that I knew now I would never be able to offer him. I couldn't let him grow up in my parents' care knowing what his mother was considered to be—to have him labelled by society because of my mistakes. He had done nothing to warrant anything other than respect, and the hope of a bright future. I made the decision that I would arrange for John's adoption at the same time as I made the arrangements for the new baby. I requested the Children's Aid Society to find a good home for John. There was no other option. To keep him any longer would have been to condemn him. Indeed, in my darkest moments I suffered pangs of guilt as to whether my decision to keep John in the first place had harmed him.

My beautiful daughter was born following the easiest delivery one could ever imagine. I had nine precious days with Mary Margaret—the name I chose to give her. Mary Margaret was brought to me for regular bottle feedings and I did my very best to avoid bonding with her. I tried to protect myself in my emotional state and dared not dwell on thoughts of her future. I did my utmost to live just for today. However, I couldn't help but be painfully aware of Mary Margaret's beauty and what an amazingly content baby she was. So much love seemed to emanate from that small bundle and I knew instinctively she would be a beautiful woman who would possess all the finer qualities that were so evident right from birth. Mary Margaret held the promise to become the woman her mother had not been capable of being—the woman her mother longed to be.

Dorothy, the girl with whom I had shared a room in the apartment, had arranged for her sister to care for my baby. I assumed that the Children's Aid Society would arrange the adoption from there. I was too caught up in my own emotional struggles to concern myself with all the details once it had been established that my baby would be in good hands. In my fragile state it was probably best that I wasn't aware of all the arrangements—it had to be a clean break. When it was time for us to leave the hospital I carried Mary Margaret in my arms to the appointed location where we were to meet the woman who would be her foster mother. There are no words adequate to describe the emotion of letting my precious daughter go from my arms knowing I would never see her or hold her ever again.

CHAPTER 9

✿

I took a room in another part of the city, as far as I could from the area where I was known. I found a job with a firm of lawyers and arranged to bring my son John to live in a foster home close by. This move led to further strife with my parents. They had, quite naturally, come to love their grandson. They chastised me for having allowed them to care for him, only to separate them now. This, in turn, caused me more doubt as to the rationality of my thinking. It also brought home the awful awareness that I seemed to be the creator of heartbreak no matter where I turned, and no matter how hard I tried to rectify my mistakes. However, I was determined. I had thought things through. I had decided. There was no turning back now.

I was able to see John regularly and take him for outings on the weekends. That all came to an abrupt end the day his adoption was arranged. From then on I lived with the heartbreaking reality that my son would be gone from my life forever.

I gathered up some photos of John's baby years, his favourite blue ducky and, along with some shinplasters and other little mementos, I placed them in a shoebox for him. I arranged to deliver them to his foster home at a time when there would be no danger of him seeing me. It was with complete confidence that I knocked at the front door. When the door was opened, from the back of the house came the scurrying of little feet and there, directly behind the foster mother, stood John. Whatever he had been told, at the sight of me his little face took on an expression of guilt. Looking as though he had done something terribly wrong, he said "oh", and turned and ran from the doorway, up the hall and out of sight. My heart cried out to him, "Oh, John, you've done nothing wrong. It is I who wronged you! You are a good boy and I love you so much—I always will!"

With the words unsaid, I delivered the little box filled with his meagre legacy and left his foster home for the last time. There had been no goodbye. I was left alone and filled with the frustration of my longing to reassure him and with the unexpressed emotion of how very much I loved him. The sight of his face with that look of unearned guilt has haunted me all these years. Remorse for that episode has been my constant companion. I should have done something, or said something, but what? I felt so helpless! The enormity of the situation still leaves me with a feeling of complete inadequacy.

Amazingly, I did eventually find some semblance of peace. Thoughts of Mary Margaret became less frequent and her image blurred in memory. John, however, was a different story. I had nursed him at my breasts, if only during his first days, and I had watched him grow from infant to toddler, to boyhood. He had a voice I could still hear. I knew his personality. I still recalled things he had said. More vividly I remembered his unconditional love and I could still feel his little arms about me!

One day shortly after his birth I had to be away for a day and I left him with my parents. It was the first time we had ever been separated. When I returned, my father met me at the door with a sombre face and told me that John didn't appear to be well. "What's wrong?" I cried as I ran toward his crib. "Oh, John, what's wrong?" At the sound of my voice, his little legs began to kick. Little hands began to move and, with a smile and the wriggling of his little body—his sheer "coming alive" at the sound of my voice—he gave us the answer to his "malady". Forgetting him was impossible. Forgetting either of them was impossible—but the memory of Mary Margaret faded more readily than did the indelible imprint of John. The memories of those years I had spent with him were to haunt me for the rest of my days.

I had never had pictures of Mary Margaret, and eventually I deliberately destroyed all my remaining photographs of John. Once they were gone, there was no turning back—just as the decision I made about the children could not be undone.

At the time of John's adoption I was working hard in an attempt to pay off the debts I had incurred through Mary Margaret's birth. I had felt too ashamed to approach the Salvation Army a second time, so had given birth in one of the city's major hospitals attended by a well-known obstetrician. This was before the nation-wide health scheme came into being. My financial burden was significant.

On one of my final visits to the attending doctor he spoke to me in a fatherly manner and provided me with some sorely needed direction. He spoke frankly. He indicated that perhaps my pregnancies had been a cry for the caring and kindness so lacking in my life. He was emphatic that I could not go on having baby after baby!

His stern lecture was delivered with my best interest at heart and I was appreciative of the fact that he was the first, and perhaps the only person, who had taken the initiative to speak so directly about unpleasant truths I had continued to skirt. His words made a difference; they helped me to face reality and make decisions. At a later date I wrote him a letter telling him so, and thanking him.

I was working several jobs at one time in order to help pay off my debts. One job was helping with the Christmas rush, clerking by day in the men's wear department of the Simpson's Store. At night I cashiered at a local cabaret—a family-owned establishment where I was also able to have my main meal of the day.

Working with me in the men's wear department was a jazz guitarist from Montreal who was on a visit home for the Christmas holidays. We became friends and, whenever I had time off, he regaled me with stories of life in La Belle Province. My father had been to Montreal many years earlier and I remembered how excitedly he had always spoken of that trip.

It was good for me to have these conversations with someone who knew nothing of my recent past. I was not being pre-judged and that paved the way to establishing friendship on solid ground. When my friend, Larry, returned to Montreal, we continued to correspond and I eventually visited the city. I knew at first sight that it was a whole different world relative to the one I had known thus far. I realized that if any city could offer a chance of escaping the ghosts of my past and making a new start, Montreal was the most likely option. Thus it was that I decided to uproot myself once again and start afresh in Montreal.

As luck would have it, one of my former workmates from the radio station where I had first worked was living in Montreal. Ronald and I had continued to correspond over the years. He was one of the few who had stood by me throughout those turbulent years. As a matter of fact, Ronald wrote me one of the most meaningful letters I have ever received. It was in response to my letter informing him of John's adoption. His letter has long since vanished, but the closing words are etched in my memory. Ronald wrote, in regard to John's proposed new family, about their love and all they could provide him with in a material sense. Ronald then continued, "offset on the other hand by the love of the most magnanimous woman he is ever likely to know and, if a married man can say this without incriminating himself, for the person you are I love you and I pray God you find your peace and happiness soon."

Ronald was still in radio, and he and his wife Louise were proud parents of a baby boy. I was invited to spend my first days in Montreal with them. I was able to find both a good job and suitable accommodation very quickly—things began to look up for me.

My first Montreal apartment was a one-room studio at the foot of Remembrance Road, the road leading up to the summit of Mount Royal. Streetcars trundled up the hill and off to the left there was a riding stable. There was a lovely open grassy knoll directly opposite my building and it was there, in full view from my picture window, that the Police put their horses through their paces each week. Montreal police still patrolled on horseback in those days and horse troughs, now planters, lined many of the major thoroughfares.

Ronald and Louise lived a short walk from my apartment building and I happily baby-sat for them whenever the need arose. Most memorable was the time their new baby's birth had become imminent and they had to hurry off to the hospital in the middle of the night. As I was less than a block from them, it was a simple matter of slipping my coat on over my pyjamas and scurrying over to spend the rest of the night on their sofa.

During my years of "exile" in Montreal, life became fuller than it had ever been. Unfortunately, it got off to a rocky start with an unfortunate marriage that ended with the honeymoon.

The bridegroom was heavily in debt, despite his well-paid job, and vowed to make the straightening out of his finances a major priority the minute we returned from a wonderful trip to New Orleans. We rented a car and drove down, giving us the opportunity to see the heartland of America on our way. New Orleans is a unique city—comparable to Montreal's uniqueness in many ways. I loved it! A charming couple we met at our motel requested a dance number to be played for us the night we all had dinner together at the Blue Room of the Roosevelt Hotel—where coast-to-coast radio broadcasts originated each week.

The first week of our return home brought reality along with it. Phone calls began several nights weekly from girls calling in response to a previous night's invitation from my husband, and I had been asleep many hours most nights before I was awakened by his footsteps coming down the hall to our room. Bills mounted at the same rate as the supply of condoms diminished, although I was not a party to either. We had agreed at the outset that it would be best to delay a family until the heavy burden of debt was under control. Condoms and diaphragms were the only choices regarding birth control, although some followed a "rhythm method" acceptable to the Church. I understood this entailed a process of taking one's temperature daily in order to ascertain fertile periods. Birth control pills were still a long way off.

We had married for the wrong reasons and without any prior counselling. I sincerely believe he sought the respectability that he mistakenly thought marriage would provide, while I had been blinded by my heart's desire to replace the family I had lost. The marriage had been consummated, but we had not lived as a married couple from that time on. At a later date I discussed details surrounding the marriage with an Anglican priest who informed me he could not consider it a valid marriage.

During this period I lost touch with Larry, my musician friend, and for a time with Ronald and Louise as well. It was only after I had time to deal with my remorse, and again recover from yet another emotional upheaval, that I began to once again pick up the pieces.

CHAPTER 10

❀

I was working for a newspaper when a handsome young Englishman arrived for an interview with the Secretary-Treasurer. My desk was strategically placed so that visitors had to be announced through me. The young man was soon hired and I encountered him in the smoke room from time to time. This was before the days of environmental and health issues connected with smoking. Smoking was permitted in only one location because of the fire code restrictions placed on the ancient building. Since we had spoken on the day of his interview it was only natural that we greet each another. His name was Michael.

Michael was recovering from a romance that had gone wrong. He had come to Canada on the first leg of what he had intended would be a trip around the world. Montreal was his first stop. The girl who had promised to join him had changed her mind. Michael had other heartache in his past too, so we had that in common. He knew of my unfortunate marriage, and confided unhappy incidents of his past. Perhaps we both saw comforting the other as a means of self-comfort. Perhaps it was the ticking of the biological clock that prompted us but, in any event, we were married immediately my divorce became final—thirteen months following my previous marriage. Once again it was a form of civil ceremony without any prior counselling. Michael was a good man with the highest principles and, moreover, possessed that keen sense of humour for which the Brits are famous.

Michael and I were married one Friday evening immediately after work and had kept our wedding a secret. It all seemed so romantic—and such fun seeing the looks on co-workers faces when they found out on Monday morning. We planned a belated honeymoon to visit his family in Britain several months hence. The honeymoon was idyllic. His mother operated a Pub in a small English Village. The George was a three-hundred-year-old coaching station and the upstairs room where we stayed was filled with priceless history. The villagers were warm and welcoming, as was Nan—Michael's mother. I fell into her arms and loved her dearly from that first moment. Half the village, it seemed, was related to Michael—what a contrast from my small family with no known relatives. I was ecstatic. For a part of the time we toured the West Country—such a picturesque part of England—and stayed a few days with Michael's dearest friends in Wimbledon. It was a wonderful trip and it seemed we couldn't possibly be happier.

I became pregnant very soon after we arrived back from England. To say we were happy at this point would be a gross understatement. Mere words can't express my feelings at the realization. Michael had the usual first-time father jitters—while I looked forward to the baby I could raise with loving care in a real family setting. My joy knew no bounds. I had confided my past experience to Michael so he was aware of all that this pregnancy meant to me.

Thirteen months after our wedding we became the proud parents of Jacqueline. I scarcely slept a wink that night—what a turmoil of emotion! Jacqueline was feisty from the moment of birth. She had been born so quickly that her doctor, who was in the hospital at the time, didn't make it to the delivery. She fought the attendants who tried to administer the eye drops. She raged in indignation. The delivery room staff remarked on what a "spirited young lady" she was. Fortunately or unfortunately, depending upon how prepared one was to cope on any given day, this was the temperament Jacqueline continued to display throughout her developing years. Perhaps it was a blessing because she gave me little time to reflect or remember. Whenever the past did manage to creep in to my thoughts, however, there was always that inner doubt as to my qualifications to rear a daughter. I felt I owed Jacqueline a life free from the mistakes I had made—while deep within I felt so ill-equipped and inadequate.

Slowly, but surely, our marriage was beginning to unravel though neither of us recognized it at the time. In hindsight it becomes quite clear. My time and energy were completely taken up with the hyperactive bundle of energy named Jacqueline. Dealing with her intelligence and energy proved to be the most daunting and formidable task I have ever undertaken at any stage in my life—the most challenging and at the same time the most rewarding.

To say Jacqueline was hyperactive does not fully describe the situation that faced us. She was saying individual words by eight months and small sentences by a year—at the same time we thought she'd never learn to walk. We should have left well enough alone. From the moment she took her first step, she ran. To let go of Jacqueline's hand in public, or anywhere, was to court disaster—and how she hated to be held onto. There was a constant tug-of-war to keep her close by. She thought nothing of streaking down the street and into a neighbour's house before I could even get the door locked for one of our outings. If we tried to hold her too tightly in check she simply sat down wherever she happened to be and turned herself into an immovable object. I recall having to follow her, red-faced, up a Church aisle just as service had begun to retrieve her from where she stood with her arms outstretched above her head as she loudly greeted the Priest standing at the lectern.

If Jacqueline wasn't running, she was climbing. Often I caught her at the top shelf of my kitchen cupboards—nothing visible but the frilly little bottom of her training pants and a pair of chubby little legs. She had a knack of using doors, drawers and shelves as stairs. The worst came the day her father took her with him when he had some business to conduct at a fresh air camp organized for inner city children. The camp was held in a massive old building several stories high on the shores of a lake and surrounded by acres of beautifully kept grounds—just the place to let Jacqueline run and romp with the other children. When Michael heard her calling, "Hi Daddy" from what sounded to be a great distance, he was puzzled at first. Then, as he finally located the direction from which her voice was coming, he froze. Jacqueline was at the very top of the narrow metal ladder that served as a fire escape for the building. She was not only at the very top, but she was also leaning out to get a better view of him!

Michael told her to stay where she was and started up after her, not being sure for one minute that she would do so. Climbing the ladder seemed to take an eternity. Every moment he was afraid she would slip and fall—or that he would. But Jacqueline was absolutely fearless and completely unaware of the danger she was in. By the time Michael reached her, he was experiencing difficulty with vertigo and getting back down with Jacqueline in tow was no small feat.

Our son, James Michael, whom we affectionately labelled JM, was born three-and-a-half years after his big sister, and following a very difficult pregnancy. I was taken to hospital at six months with signs of premature labour and then, a week later, sent home with orders for complete bed rest. That meant being off my feet for a matter of three months. The ultimatum I was given by my doctor let us know we were in serious trouble. There was no possibility of our disobeying the instruction.

Jacqueline had stayed with a neighbour during my days in hospital. Michael brought her home each evening when he returned from work. On the Sunday afternoon he came to bring me home from the hospital, he left Jacqueline at the home of a former colleague, and we stopped there to collect her on the way home. I'm moved to tears whenever I think of the sight of the quiet little girl who greeted me. This chattering dynamo was standing stalk still and wordless. She approached me slowly, almost cautiously, before climbing up onto my lap. Without a word, she curled herself up in my arms and began to tremble. I held her close until the shaking finally subsided. It was so obvious our separation had been very traumatic for her—I felt so helpless. There was no way I could sufficiently explain the necessity of my being away from her, and no way could I avoid the separation. I was told later that during that week I was in hospital that our neighbour had taken Jacqueline to my paediatrician—Jacqueline had broken out in a skin rash. One of the doctor's first questions was, "How long has her mother been away?" Apparently the detergent my neighbour used had caused an allergic reaction, although Jacqueline was not given to allergies. I felt so badly—all the more so, knowing that in a few short months there would be a separation once again. By the time of the second occurrence, however, Jacqueline appeared to have become accustomed to being distanced from me.

Michael, with the help of generous neighbours, was able to cope with the demands of running the household and caring for Jacqueline during my months of bed rest. My constant companion during those long days was a stray kitten we had taken in—Louis. Louis was content to just lie curled up on my burgeoning tummy for hours on end. At times, by his patience and devotion, I felt he might even be the reincarnation of Toodles.

Finally, after seemingly endless weeks, I was once again admitted to hospital. After being in such a rush to come into the world, JM had apparently changed his mind and was in no hurry at all to be born. As he was growing at an alarming rate by this time, my doctor decided to help him along. It was a long and difficult delivery but it was worth every moment when he was finally placed in my arms.

What a placid baby he was. JM loved to be cuddled and he was such a joy to care for. Here was a baby I could hold and rock and sing to instead of one who wriggled and strained to be free of any arms. Unlike his sister, JM would "snuggle in" when he was held. When he cried he did so without raging, and during his waking moments calmly studied the world around him. He appeared to approach life far more cautiously than had his sister who gave the impression of traveling in a mini cyclone.

JM was fifteen months old when I finally admitted to an ever-deepening depression. My happiness should have been complete, but I was merely going through the motions. It was several years before these issues were to be resolved, and several more after that before there was any chance at normalcy in the household.

I was barely finished my treatment when Jacqueline became seriously ill and was diagnosed with a complicated and life-threatening case of mononucleosis—her liver and spleen both were enlarged to the point of rupture. I had strict orders to see that she had a no-fat and high-sugar diet in order to protect her liver and, in addition, to maintain complete bed rest. It wasn't difficult for me to keep Jacqueline still for the weeks she was confined to bed—she recalled later that she felt too tired to even lie there.

Within that same year JM contracted viral meningitis. His doctor felt it would be better for him to be at home with me rather than in a hospital setting—since it was aseptic there was no medication to be administered. Fortunately, he was still small enough for me to carry to the toilet during the days when his legs were too twisted with paralysis to support him. The virus eventually ran its course and JM was once again his normal self with no apparent effects of his illness other than the fact he was terribly underweight. Coincidentally, he had decided on his own to become a vegetarian—although, as a five-year-old I think the idea was more that he had simply decided he didn't want to eat any of the cute little animals like those he saw on TV. I cooked special meals for JM, supplementing the family fare with nutritious yet highly caloric dishes especially for him. I managed to put fourteen pounds back on his overly slender frame and soon JM was once again the picture of health.

CHAPTER 11

❀

That's not to say there were no happy times for us. On the contrary, there were many. While the children were still quite young we invested in a tent trailer and spent long holiday weekends at lovely wooded campsites throughout Vermont, New Hampshire and Maine. On our three-week summer vacations we ventured further afield. At various times we camped our way throughout the entire eastern seaboard of the United States—through Virginia, the Carolinas, Georgia and over to Michigan. We also did Canada from coast to coast—from the shores of the Pacific off Vancouver Island to the shores of the Atlantic off the coast of Newfoundland.

Of all our adventures, Newfoundland had to be the most memorable for me. We crossed on the overnight ferry and it was nearing eight in the morning when we had our first sighting of the rockbound coast of Newfoundland. What a dramatic sight it was!

As we drove onto land at Port aux Basques and proceeded through the Long Range Mountains, we were totally overwhelmed by the powerful impact of the rugged scenery. We soon discovered that the beauty of the land was matched by the warmth of its people. We had never met with such generosity—not only of spirit, but of worldly possessions as well. The Newfoundlanders we met were not materially wealthy but, whatever they did have, they were happy to share.

We had been camping at Corner Brook. It was time to move on and Michael was busy securing our little flat-bottomed boat to the trailer. Suddenly the hook slipped out of his wet hands and flew upward, shattering the lens of his glasses into his right eye. I told the children to run quickly to the Ranger's Station about a mile up the road, while I dampened tissues at the nearby pump and did my best to gently blot loose shards of glass from the eye—which I insisted he hold open with both hands. I was afraid that blinking his eye might cause further abrasions. By the time I had done all I could, the Ranger had arrived with his truck and, while Michael was being settled, only then did I become aware of the pain that gripped the pit of my stomach. I stepped to the side of the campsite and bent over with my arms hugging my middle and trembled uncontrollably for the few moments it took to regain my composure.

It was twenty miles to the nearest hospital and when we finally arrived we were seen almost immediately. The doctor did the best he could with cleansing the eye and placed a bandage over it. He would accept no payment.

When the Ranger drove us back to the camp, he helped us unload and set up our tent once again. There was no way Michael could drive. His perception of distance had been compromised by having the use of only one eye. He realized this later that afternoon when it took him ages to pick a few wild raspberries for dinner. Each berry took several attempts before he could actually grasp it. None of them were where they appeared to be at first glance.

We were just finishing our dinner that evening when a car pulled up and a young woman came to our tent. She had come to inform us that an eye specialist would be at the hospital the following day. She asked that we be there at ten next morning to see him. We were dumbfounded to think that she had driven forty miles round trip to inform us of the appointment!

Thanks to the Ranger, we once again made the trip to the hospital. The specialist said that the eye was doing nicely and we were relieved to learn there would be no serious consequence from the mishap. After several days we were able to be on our way, believing that the worst was behind us, and looking forward to the rest of our holiday.

Gros Morne national park was something out of a picture book. Such unspoiled land—the plateau of the mountain ended in a sheer drop to the Fjord below. There was a long trek across a deserted field to Western Brook Pond that we were told would give us a spectacular view of the Fjord and the towering sheer cliffs. We started off, noting that there were tall twigs set out at intervals along the way. Actually, the field was a bog. We were not certain but we assumed the markings denoted unstable conditions, so we carefully avoided those areas.

We were nearly halfway across the half-mile or so distance when suddenly my left foot went through the crust of the earth and plunged deeper and deeper until I was in well over my knee. Michael said, "Try to keep your boot on when you pull your foot out." I looked him directly in the eye as I said in a very quiet voice, "I would be happy to be able to pull my foot up with or without my boot."

At that, adrenalin began to rush and, with his arms around me under the armpits, Michael pulled with an almost superhuman strength until I was standing once again—with both boots—beside him and my wide-eyed children.

There was some question at that point as to whether we would continue on or go back. I felt since we were halfway to either point that we should carry on to see the promised spectacular view that had brought us there. At that moment the children, almost in unison, pointed to my feet exclaiming, "Mom, look!" As we stood there discussing which way to go, I had been slowly sinking into the bog and an inch or so of me had already disappeared below the surface. There was no time to bicker over which way to go. The only alternative was to move, and move we did toward our original destination. It was truly the promised spectacular view, and worth every frightening moment getting there.

When we eventually arrived back at the populated area, we searched out the Ranger's station and reported our incident, hoping to spare some other unsuspecting tourist a similar experience. They were very kind and took full particulars. Then, to add some levity to the situation, the Ranger inquired if we had noticed any hats floating nearby!

A ferry strike was looming. Our vacation was almost at an end and the children were due to start back to school. We were nearing the dock at Argentia when news of the strike was announced, and it promised to be a long one. We turned around and found a campground where we settled down to wait. We were among the fortunate ones. Many of the cars that followed ours to Argentia, as well as many who had chosen to return via Port aux Basques, were stuck in bumper-to-bumper traffic with no way out. This was a situation that would exist until the strike came to an end. We heard stories on the radio of Newfoundlanders bringing these people into their homes, providing them with food and clothing and even putting them up in their own beds while they themselves slept on cots, sofas—wherever they could find. Many of the stranded were American tourists who could not believe the generosity of the Newfoundlanders and, when interviewed on local radio, they were hard pressed to know how they could ever begin to repay such a great debt of kindness.

We camped beside a little trout stream but were unable to catch any fish. We had to rely on the supermarkets for our food but, when we saw how rapidly the stocks were being depleted—with no new supplies able to get over from the mainland—we felt guilty about shopping for food. We drove to a fishing dock to buy cod from the fishing boats as they came in. I selected a beautiful twelve-pound black cod to bake on the campfire coals. The fisherman would take no money. He recognized us as stranded tourists and with a wave of his hand said, "That's all right" in his thick Newfie accent. We learned to eat Hardtack and Brewis and created a substantial soup using turkey necks. It was nearly another two weeks before we finally left that rugged bit of paradise, taking with us enough memories to last a lifetime. Rather than leaving a boot, I found I had left a part of my heart.

CHAPTER 12

❁

When the day finally dawned that I could no longer cope with my deepening depression, I was forced to seek help. At the time I entered treatment I had begun having recurring dreams. No matter what the circumstance, these dreams always began with my husband Michael and ended with him becoming my mother. The two always blended into one. Then there were sometimes dreams where I was entirely alone in a vast area of barren landscape—sometimes it was a glacier of icy snow, and at other times an expanse of parched earth lacking any vegetation. Whatever the dream, it always had the same devastating emotional impact.

Eventually I was forced to deal some inevitable truths and then, much later, to finally recognize the person I was under all the emotional baggage I had accumulated over a lifetime. I began, for the first time, to know who I was and to see things as they were.

I appeared be the victim of psychological abuse—not intentional, of course. I can't honestly believe that Michael could intend such a thing. Nonetheless, he had unwittingly been reinforcing my weaknesses and I had played directly into the scheme of things. The situation had evolved over a period of years and it was on those grounds that I eventually felt compelled to file for divorce.

My lawyer was visibly distressed when she saw the judge who entered the courtroom to preside that day. He had a reputation for being very tough and, with no witness to speak in my defence, she felt my case was all but lost—she anticipated losing her first case. The only doctor who could give credence to my situation had gone to practice in another province and the only neighbour I might have called upon had also moved elsewhere. In keeping with my nature, I had kept my problems closely guarded from the community.

I cited examples of my husband's behaviour and how they affected me. I had lost twenty-five pounds as a direct result of our marital breakdown. The weight loss was not difficult to believe as I stood before the judge as an almost skeletal figure.

I spoke from the heart. It was the only ammunition I had but it carried the ring of truth. I felt utter hopelessness for my welfare and the unhappy thought of remaining in the marriage was more than sufficient for the judge to grant my petition, without hesitation.

I have tried many times to understand the breakdown and what I perceived to be Michael's hostile treatment toward me. Although he seemed proud of me in public, in private I felt his sarcasm—or was met with silence.

Each time I perceived myself to be rebuffed, a part of my consciousness reverted back to episodes in my childhood. Once when I had unwittingly rested my hand on my mother's back as she bent over to retrieve something from the oven, she had cried harshly, "Don't touch my back!" Startled, I asked why her back hurt and her response was simply, "You did that to me." Whether I was aware she was referring to my birth, or whether it was the manner in which her words were spoken, it was one more childhood mystery I did not pursue. Perhaps I harboured a fear of what her answer might be. But I held the hurt of that rebuff deep within, along with many others.

When confronted with examples of his sarcasm, Michael denied them. Things were always relegated to the realm of my imagination. Little by little I had begun feeling once again like the unworthy little girl whose mother had been forced to hit her for reasons unknown. Obviously a loving mother wouldn't hit her daughter for no reason; similarly, a caring husband wouldn't hurt his wife. I was not consciously aware of my regression into this state but I had begun to accept myself as unfit to be treated differently.

I've come to realize in life that we inadvertently search out the people who complement our inner perception of ourselves and, although Michael was a good person, his unconscious behaviour toward me fuelled my deep-rooted feeling that I deserved such treatment. The only thing that prevented me from slipping even further into that cloud of sombre depression was my fear for my children's future.

It was indeed that apprehension for my children's future that served as the catalyst for change, prompting me to finally seek immediate professional advice. That decision was made the day I stood looking at the suitcases we kept stored beneath the stairs—wondering how I could go anywhere without money. There was no access to day-care in those days, and we were three thousand miles from the nearest relative. The problem of finding suitable care for the children while I went out to work put me at a total impasse—with no means of escape. I was engulfed by a feeling of utter hopelessness and despair when, suddenly, there was a glimmer of realization. For a fleeting moment a solution occurred to me. I could end it all—taking the children with me. I recoiled in horror to think I had actually conceived such an idea and knew at that moment it was time to seek immediate help.

I was to discover that depression is the flip side of the coin; the other side is anger. I was unable to allow myself to be angry with my husband just as I had been unable to allow myself to hate my mother, because neither instance would have been deemed as "acceptable" behaviour in my mind. Hence, depression took over.

I began to understand that my mother had also been a victim and that she had, undoubtedly, suffered much. I learned to feel compassion for her and discovered that, despite all, I did love her and had been deeply hurt by her betrayal. This was a sad fact that I simply had to learn to accept. I'm so grateful I had the opportunity later to tell her that I loved her.

It was several years before my treatment finally came to an end and I had acquired a new inward perception of myself. It was necessary to allow this newly found "me" to gain strength—to forge my identity and, at last, to put the past to rest. Without Michael's complete understanding of the situation, as well as his support, my progress would be very difficult if not impossible. It was at this juncture, on one of my last appointments, that my doctor expressed a desire to see us both. During that final consultation Michael was asked at one point why he had just spoken to me "with that note of sarcasm". He apparently had not been aware, and denied it, but the doctor had detected it. It was during this same appointment that Michael was asked to come back alone the following week. I felt optimistic that we were on the road to happiness at last.

It was all-important for Michael to see how his behavior was interrelated with the problems I had incurred. There was no blame to be laid—simply an understanding of what was happening between us so we might work together on a solution.

When the following week came, Michael stated that he wouldn't keep the appointment—he didn't need to. It had been my problem and, if I felt I had finally worked things through, then that was it. My hopes were dashed. We should have been facing the future as a couple, yet there I was feeling totally alone and once again at an impasse. Not only had we reached an impasse, but at the same time I felt I had been left with a clear message that my well being and future health were of lesser importance than his personal reluctance to visit a psychiatrist. I had the feeling our last door of opportunity had been slammed shut. An even wider chasm began to stretch between us.

I was not yet confident enough to stand up to the test on my own. My only safety seemed to lie in avoidance. Unfortunately, shutting myself away from Michael caused me to distance myself from my children as well, for they quite naturally involved themselves in family activities that included their father and should have included me.

I began to feel guilt at posing as a family unit to the community, all the while knowing the domestic rift was ever widening. I dreaded the possibility of a twenty-fifth wedding celebration just a few short years away. How could we in all honesty "celebrate?" The situation as it was did not equate a marriage in any real sense of the word—to accept congratulations for having survived those many years would be dishonest.

The children had grown and the prospect of an "empty nest" loomed ominously. How very empty it would be inhabited by two people who had become strangers. Self-preservation led me to finally go my separate way. I sincerely felt that to remain any longer would have caused me to be caught once again in a downward spiral. One can't successfully maintain the *status quo*. One either continues to grow or there is regression. There's no standing still. In later years I often wondered what our future might have held if Michael had kept the appointment that my doctor had requested.

Once again I was starting over! Now, at a point in time when I should have been looking forward to that "empty nest" that would have provided us the time to concentrate on ourselves and prepare for our "golden years", I found myself job hunting. I would need an income to live apart from Michael. I didn't propose to sue for any sort of alimony. Jacqueline was already sharing an apartment with friends and had a temporary job, but JM was still at home—though anxiously awaiting his next birthday so he too could strike out on his own. Any kind of settlement would have meant selling the house. Laws were not yet in place to divide assets equitably, nor were there laws regarding automatic divorce following a required separation period.

I wanted JM and Jacqueline to have the stability of the family home, at least. Michael had always worked hard and provided well for his family; he too, deserved to be left with his home in tact. My concern was my quality of life, and that to me only meant inner peace and happiness; no amount of money could buy that. I felt in my heart that Michael would be happier, too, once the initial separation had been dealt with.

I managed to find a wonderful job with an international organization. It was interesting beyond belief. Suddenly I was in touch with all corners of the world—in contact with places whose names had formerly been merely words in a newspaper. Days at work flew by. I used some of my first pay cheques to file for an order allowing me to leave the common domicile. Without this I could have been sued for desertion. Subsequent pay cheques allowed me to save enough money to pay the legal costs of the divorce.

I found a lovely little studio apartment in a good location and at a reasonable rent. It was one room with an equipped kitchenette, and the building featured a bright and spacious laundry room on the main floor. It was a cosy nest and I enjoyed it once I had managed to stem the tears of regret. Once again I had proven myself a failure and caused heartache to others. There was much work for me to do learning to forgive myself and to become the person I was meant to be—the one who had lost sight of herself so many, many years earlier.

One room meant very little to buy in the way of furniture so, with a little ingenuity, I was able to decorate and furnish with very little expense. I enjoyed it immensely, despite the pangs of loneliness. My daughter Jacqueline was living further up the street. We visited each other and I did all I could to bridge the gap I felt had grown between us. JM, though still at home with his father, came to visit me every Sunday afternoon. When I had managed to put some money aside, I took him for a week's vacation to Disney World. Unfortunately the weather was frightful—bitterly cold for Florida—but we had the time together and shared some lasting memories.

Gradually our lives began to take on a feeling of normalcy. Within a few years following our divorce, Michael remarried. Prior to his marriage, however, we had begun to accept each other as friends. Michael had a keen sense of humour that served him well. His company was pleasant when there was no longer a tug-of-war between us. I enjoyed our occasional outings to a concert or theatre with mutual friends—even a family get-together at Christmas one year. That all ended, of course, when he remarried.

In hindsight, I wonder if the terrible heartbreak of a failed marriage might have been avoided if we had taken the time to know each other better before we took the plunge. Perhaps in getting to know each other better our symbiotic relationship might have revealed itself more clearly and might have prevented us from going any further. I can't bring myself to speculate on that aspect, however, because had we not married we wouldn't have had the blessing of parenting two wonderful children. I can't imagine life without them!

It took me several years but I did finally become financially able to graduate to a three-room apartment. At last I was able to roll up the exercise mat I'd been sleeping on and relegate it to a closet. I was finally going to have a bed, and a bedroom as well—what luxury. My new kitchen was even large enough to accommodate a table, and the living room was large enough for a drop-leaf table that could be opened up whenever I had guests for dinner. I was feeling such a sense of accomplishment and contentment with my lot, when—out of the blue—I won a trip to Switzerland!

I had never in my wildest dreams imagined myself going to continental Europe. I had, of course, visited England and Wales with Michael on our Honeymoon to meet his family and friends, and several times later with the children.

I took some of my savings and arranged to extend my trip to include Southern Germany, Austria and Northern Italy, as well. It was a single ticket that I had won, but I had no qualms about going on the guided tours on my own. I had become quite accustomed to my solitary existence.

CHAPTER 13

The week before I was booked to leave for Switzerland, I had only a few last-minute arrangements to make which included getting an early flu shot. I would be away for a month and by that time we would be well into the flu season. I called my doctor and arranged to have my shot that evening on the way home from work. Afterwards I had intended to do some shopping but, when I arrived at the store, I felt unusually tired so I decided to go home and have an early night instead. There was a Working Paper that had to be finished next morning for a scheduled meeting and I had planned to go in to work a little earlier than usual to attend to it. I felt achy when I awoke next morning so I took a pain killer. I had to be at my best in order to cope with the heavy workload I had facing me.

I was in my office early and working at my computer before anyone else had arrived. I had to stop typing quite frequently to rub my palms—they were so itchy. So was my chin! I was concentrating on the task at hand but had a vague awareness of being annoyed by the itching. Then the phone rang and, exasperated, I walked over to answer it. I realized I was unsteady on my feet—and I had a strange feeling in the pit of my stomach. As I put the receiver to my ear and endeavoured to speak, it dawned on me my words were, for the most part, unintelligible—my tongue seemed to be swollen. Everything was suddenly happening very quickly and by the time I had hung up the receiver I realized I was in some kind of serious trouble. The strange sensation in my stomach had begun to feel like a vice gripping my middle. I was dizzy and staggered as I tried to walk. I felt nauseous and light-headed—my vision was distorted. Thinking I was about to throw up, I lurched my way to the ladies' room just around the corner from my office. I peered at myself in the mirror and through the blur could see a red, swollen face that I presumed was mine although it bore no resemblance to the face I was accustomed to seeing.

Not being certain whether I was going to throw up or faint, I went out into the hall and immediately encountered my Chief who was just arriving. He was always one of the first in to the office every morning and, luckily for me, that morning was no exception. I blurted out that something was radically wrong—that I wasn't sure if I was going to pass out. Taken totally off guard, he stared at me and all he could blurt out was, "Your face is all swollen." "You'd better get to the nurse!"

How I got to the nurse's office I'm not sure. I recall I encountered colleagues on my way but who they were or what was said is anyone's guess. It seemed my luck was holding—the nurse had just arrived that moment. That's when things became a bit frantic because the nurse really wasn't certain what to do with me. She phoned the company doctor who told her to give me some Benedryl. This was probably a good idea, but it turned out to be impossible for me to swallow the pill, much less drink the water I was given to wash it down.

By this time my Chief had recovered from the shock of the sight that greeted him upon his arrival that morning and had come to the nurse's office accompanied by Marie, my friend and colleague who affectionately called me Mom. Marie had apparently arrived for work and had gone to make coffee while I was in the ladies' room. She knew I was in the office because she had noticed the work on my computer screen. When Marie returned to her desk, she was told of my situation and insisted on seeing me. To add levity to the very worrisome situation she remarked to me, "It's not safe for a person to turn her back long enough to make a cup of coffee around this place!"

It was obvious by this time that I was hospital bound. Marie ran back to the office for our handbags and coats and was back at the nurse's office by the time the ambulance attendants were getting me on to the stretcher. By the time they arrived I was stomping my feet on the floor in an attempt to stop their incessant itching.

Marie insisted on coming in the ambulance with me to the hospital. She sat up front and my stretcher was parked at curbside while the rear doors were being opened. A colleague arriving for work saw me and, without a word, came over and kissed my cheek. I can't convey the meaning that silent gesture held for me. It's a moment I'll never forget.

En route to the hospital I shared my stretcher with an oxygen tank although it didn't have to be put to use. It seemed that my breathing was the only thing about me that appeared normal. The ambulance attendant asked me a number of health-related questions as we sped along with the siren blaring. My negative response to the entire list prompted him to say, "You're in perfect health." Despite the seriousness of my condition, I couldn't resist the temptation to quip, "If I'm in such perfect health, then why are you carting me away in an ambulance?"

I was deposited in the emergency ward of the nearest hospital—in a bed immediately in front of the nurse's station—and was hooked up to an array of equipment. I could hear my heartbeat beeping somewhere above my bed. I couldn't fail to be impressed how quickly things were accomplished. My clothing, that had taken me such a while to put on that morning, had come off all at once with one swift movement. When I glanced at the clock directly ahead of me I noticed that only twenty minutes had elapsed since I last noted the time while still working at the office.

I was being medicated intravenously but things appeared to be worsening despite repeated assurances that I'd begin to feel better soon. Terrible chills came over me in waves and seemed to penetrate every fibre of my being. I shivered uncontrollably and nothing, it seemed—not even the heated blankets that covered me—could warm me. I dreaded the onslaught of each new icy wave, and with each moment of relief between them I could feel myself becoming measurably weaker.

It was only after my stomach had been flushed out (thanks to copious amounts of saline solution administered by Marie) that my condition finally began to turn around. Even so, I was kept in that bed by the nursing station despite other emergencies including an underground fire and badly burned firefighters. It was only later in the day that I was finally relegated to a bed further up the line and then, eventually, to a quieter recovery area away from the "field of action" and where some of the patients were sitting up and reading books.

Marie had gone back to the office as soon as it appeared certain my condition had begun to improve. She returned to the hospital to take me home. While I was being discharged the stern warning I had already been given by the attending physician, as well as one of the nurses, was repeated. I had been very lucky to survive. The doctor went so far as to say that, since my first anaphylactic reaction had been so severe, there could be no guarantee a second time. I would have to be extremely careful from now on.

I was discharged with a supply of cortisone tablets to take with decreasing frequency, along with very strict orders regarding future medications. I was also given an appointment to see an Allergist in order to determine exactly what sensitivities managed to confuse my immune system and turn my own body into "the enemy".

My scheduled trip to Switzerland was only a week away. I had planned and looked forward to the trip for too long. Although my system was still a bit unsettled and I was still shaken by the suddenness and the severity of my medical emergency, I was determined to make the trip. Seven days later I was on my way.

Although I had won a single economy flight to Switzerland, when I went to pick up the ticket I was pleasantly surprised to find I had been bumped up to business class. I was also given a letter inviting me to use the facilities of the Hospitality Suite when I arrived at the airport.

Swissair could not have been more hospitable. The meals, wine, and in-flight service were *par excellence.* When I arrived at the hotel I had booked through my travel agent, I was delighted to see that the TV in my room had been left on and there, in big letters across the screen, I saw my name and a message of welcome. I was thrilled!

Switzerland is a country that prides itself on the quality of its chocolate, and well they should. I will always remember the enormous glass bowl at the end of the reception desk—filled to the brim with a variety of little individually wrapped bars. It was a wonderful assortment just waiting for passers-by to help themselves. A detour past that bowl was on my agenda whenever I entered or left the Lobby.

I spent my first day acquainting myself with Zurich. What a charming city. I fell in love with it instantly. The following day I had signed up for an organized tour. It included a bus ride around the city to various points of interest followed by a trip to Rapperswill, a lovely old historic place. From Rapperswill we returned to Zurich by boat—a two-hour ride. Our tour of Switzerland began the following day. Helen and Phil, a lovely couple from Toronto, befriended me almost immediately. It later turned out that they were the only other people out of the whole busload of tourists who had arranged, as had I, to take the Glacier Express from Zermatt to St. Moritz. It was so much nicer having someone to share the journey although Helen, unfortunately, was suffering some kind of upper respiratory infection and was not her usually bright self. In fact, she was quite ill. It was a long trip—from early morning until well after night fall—which was unfortunate because as dusk closed in, visibility diminished. Every inch of the scenery was breathtakingly beautiful but eventually there was nothing but darkness outside the train window. We arrived at St. Moritz in complete darkness.

While at Zermatt we had seen the full grandeur of the Alps and been so close to the Matterhorn we almost felt we could reach out and touch the peak. I am certain the Alps are breathtaking at any time but to someone who so recently had a brush with death, the sight of them was a true gift from God. I had never felt so alive nor had I ever appreciated anything so much. The trip I had looked forward to so eagerly became a trip of gigantic proportion—appreciated in a manner unlike anything before. Life had taken on a whole new meaning for me and I looked at everything through fresh eyes.

At the end of the week when the Switzerland tour came to an end, I bid adieu to the tour group and my friends Helen and Phil. I boarded a train in Lucerne bound for Frankfurt, Germany. Fortunately, I had a day in Frankfurt before my next tour began—I was ill. I displayed all of Helen's flu-like symptoms that had prevented her from properly enjoying the Glacier Express ride. Spending the day in close confinement with her on the train must have given me the bug. I spent the day in bed in my hotel room. That evening there was an orientation dinner scheduled for the tour group. I managed to join in long enough to hear what the tour guide had to say and then went back to bed. Bright and early next morning we were on the bus and it was all I could do to sit upright. Any protection I had been given by the fateful flu shot had obviously been washed away with the saline solution that had totally flooded my system and cleansed me of everything.

From Frankfurt we traveled the Romantic Road through Southern Germany, and then through Austria to Vienna. By this time I was beginning to feel human again. Finally we headed down through Northern Italy before making a loop of Switzerland. This time I was doing the circuit in reverse. However, we stayed at different hotels and saw some new sights along with the now familiar ones. I also omitted the Glacier Express run. Wendy, a friendly girl from Australia, was also a lone traveller and we teamed up for many of the activities. It was Wendy who came to Frankfurt train station to see me off when the tour ended and I returned at last to Zurich. Wendy and I corresponded for a number of years following our adventures together but somehow we eventually lost contact.

I loved Zurich and was so glad I had decided to stay a few days extra after the end of the tours. I stayed at the same hotel I had visited when I first arrived. This time the message on my TV screen bade me "Wilkomen back Ruth Lester."

I had a marvellous time exploring the city. There appeared to be a lot of wealth in Zurich. Everything, it seemed, was of the highest quality and beautifully arranged. The city is spotless. I was amazed to find cut flowers in the public washrooms near the train station—a lovely fresh bouquet at each sink. I came to the conclusion I must look like a native. Everywhere I turned people were asking me questions. When I spoke to them in English they looked shocked—even a panhandler whom I encountered near the entrance to the little park allocated for drug users.

German seemed to be the predominant language in the country although there are French and Italian divisions as well. Whenever I was unable to find anyone who spoke English, I resorted to my limited French and that seemed to serve me well.

I left Switzerland totally hooked on muesli, duvets, and café au lait. And it was some time after my arrival back in Montreal before I stopped walking into doors. My month in Europe was just long enough for me to become accustomed to having doors part quickly as I approached them. We tend to think of North America as the "new world"—a more modernized way of life. I must confess I found much of Europe's "old world" charm to be a step ahead of us!

It was a wonderful trip and, for obvious reasons, the trip of a lifetime. I knew my life could never be the same again. God had spared me and I vowed that I would live each day from then on to the fullest. There was obviously something more that I was intended to accomplish on this earth and I bided my time, ever mindful that I still had unfinished work to do. Whatever the work might be was still to be determined.

CHAPTER 14

✿

Almost immediately after I returned to Montreal from my trip to the Alpine countries, I was offered a five-and-a-half room apartment at a price I could afford. It was spacious—in fact, the entry hall was almost as large as the living room had been in my three-room apartment. It was a square entry hall and large enough to be furnished. Straight ahead there was a large walk-in closet and the doorway to the kitchen. On the right was a smaller hall leading to the bedrooms and an archway that was the entrance to the living room that featured a large picture window with an unobstructed view. Along one of the living room walls was a beautiful ornate fireplace, still in working condition. Opposite the fireplace was an archway to the dining room. The dining room was separated from the kitchen by a swinging door. The kitchen was large and easily doubled as family room with a small table and chairs, a bookcase, and TV. It was a perfect spot for me to read the paper or glance through cookbooks, do my telephoning and catch up on the evening news while I prepared my dinner. The apartment was in an up-scale neighbourhood with wonderful shopping and excellent transportation. A bonus, too, was that it was on the second floor with a view leading to Mount Royal—a spectacular view. The seventy-year old building had high ceilings, lending the air of spaciousness found in a self-contained cottage rather than an apartment

In truth, I felt I had at last arrived at the place where my searching could end. This apartment was a home in every sense of the word, and it was the place I felt I'd be happy for the rest of my days. I had loved decorating each of my apartments, but this one lent itself beautifully to some major undertakings—I was ecstatic and immediately set out to incorporate them.

I was officially retired now although I continued working from time-to-time on short-term contracts. I also worked three afternoons a week maintaining a database for an organization dealing with business aviation. I had time to enjoy my new home and I had sufficient income to take advantage of special travel arrangements offered occasionally through my former employer. I was fortunate enough to spend ten days in Russia and to visit China on two separate occasions—but that's sufficient material for another book.

I had been working three afternoons a week for several years before Washington made the decision to close the Montreal office. We were devastated. However, the silver lining of that dark cloud was the fact that much of the office equipment was not worth transporting to the United States. The computers were outdated from a technological standpoint, although still in excellent condition. I was more than happy to be allowed to take mine home. I also took the small desk it stood on but refused my larger desk. My apartment was large, but not large enough to accommodate that huge item.

Having a computer at home soon led me to arrange for an Internet provider and to get myself on-line. I had no idea at the time what an important part of my life e-mail was to become. I had heard people talking about corresponding with friends and family on the other side of the world but couldn't think of anyone whom I would want to contact. I really didn't expect to find much use for the feature, but was soon to discover otherwise. Having retired from an international organization, I had worked with people from every corner of the globe. As they reached retirement age, they were required to return immediately to their own administrations. Generally, they were not Canadian citizens or landed immigrants, but rather working by special arrangement in our country. Almost immediately my address book began filling with names of friends and colleagues with whom I might not have otherwise kept in touch if this had required letters or phone calls. A few lines by e-mail now and again proved to be the perfect way to keep in touch.

It must have been well before my move to my new apartment that my son, John, had embarked on a mission to find his birth mother. He registered with the Adoption Disclosure Registry and was put on what was to be a twelve-year waiting list before files would be opened to him. However, upon registration he was informed that non-identifying records indicated he had a full-blood sister who had been placed for adoption at birth. John's adoptive parents had told him his birth name so he was able to search for me on his own. However, his sister's name was a mystery. John travelled in the general location of his birthplace, rooted through libraries, joined Parent Finders and registered with several other databases as well.

Months turned into years and one by one the trails ran cold. John was pretty much resigned to the fact that his was a lost cause and that he might never manage to locate his mother much less his sister. It was at that point that Mary Margaret registered with the same agency and John was informed. Although John knew of her existence, she had no idea she had a brother. Neither adoptive family had been made aware at the time of the adoptions that there was another child that had been separated from its sibling.

A match having been made, the Agency set about negotiating a contact between the two. Mary Margaret's adoptive parents had changed her name. She was now known as Cynthia Anne, shortened to Cindy. Some of the bureaucracy was circumvented and the reunion process was accelerated. John contacted Cindy by phone and, within a week, they were face-to-face in Cindy's home—little more than an hour's drive away from John's home. Meeting his sister held incredible meaning for John but to Cindy, who had no previous knowledge of a brother, the moment was indescribable.

The result of that reunion had far-reaching effects. There were many coincidences in their lives. Most ironically, the two adoptive fathers grew up in the same town, went to the same school, graduated from the same class in high school, and went on to study at the same university. They adopted one child each—without knowing of the other's similar decision—and raised them in communities that were a mere half-hour drive apart. Sadly, both adoptive fathers had died by the time John and Cindy met so the two men never knew how much more they had in common than their schooling.

Within four months' time, some eighty surprised and delighted guests attended a garden party in honour of their official meeting. The party was hosted by John's brother, Gordon—a very caring brother who exemplified the wonderful family that John had been adopted into. The invitees wore either a pink or a blue nametag bearing a baby photo of the sibling they knew. To their amazement, many sported both colours before the day was through. Their respective adoptive families had friends in common. Many had known both John and Cindy, yet never realized there was a connection between the two. They had travelled similar paths in parallel with each other for their entire lives, even narrowly missing attending the same school! It was an amazing portrayal of how much stranger truth is than fiction.

Shortly after meeting John, Cindy shed pound after pound and trimmed down to a very neatly proportioned size. She adored her brother as he did her and the two became inseparable. Cindy explained her weight loss as a cessation of overeating to compensate for something that was missing in her life and, as John put it, "We're a package deal—accept us both or have none." Since the reunion, the two adoptive families have entwined and become relatives as surely as if the siblings' common blood flowed throughout them all.

Meeting Cindy sparked in John a whole new enthusiasm for searching for me once again. Cindy was a newcomer to the search process and, with traditional beginner's luck, she found a gold mine of photos in a high school yearbook. At last they knew what their mother looked like and together they set out to follow every new lead in order to find her.

By this time, the time restriction was over and the Adoptive Disclosure Registry was free to divulge the information they had on file for John. Here, in part, is how it described me at the time of the adoptions:

"Your birth mother … was 5'6" tall and weighed 125 lbs. She was said to be very attractive, typically Irish in her appearance having dark naturally curly hair, dark brown sparkling eyes and a clear complexion. She was described as a sensitive, affectionate, dramatic, well-poised person of above average intelligence. She was capable, independent and always well groomed. She enjoyed reading factual material and magazines. Your birth mother was an only child. Her parents expected a great deal from her and it was very difficult for them to understand their daughter. Your birth mother appeared to be starved for affection. She was described as an affectionate type of girl, highly emotional and sensitive. It appeared her parents neglected her and have not given her any understanding, particularly during the past few years."

Since John and Cindy had already located numerous pictures of me, there was very little new material once the file was released. They also found newspaper clippings and pictures of their father. They established that he had married about the time that Cindy had been born, that he and his wife had never had children, and that he had died several years previously.

Once again the trail ran cold and, when it became evident that even the Adoption Disclosure Registry had been unsuccessful in its search, John was ready to call it quits. As there were no records found of my death, and none indicating I was still resident in Canada, it was surmised that I had possibly moved to another part of the world. It would appear that Quebec fell into that category, as far as record sharing is concerned, for it appeared that all information came to an abrupt halt at the Ontario/Quebec border. Most certainly my marriages were recorded and would have borne my maiden name. Additionally, income taxes filed before my marriage would also have borne my maiden name, as well as various employment records. Cindy was adamant they not give up the search.

Ironically, I was in Windsor the day John and Cindy were there hunting for clues as to my whereabouts. It's not an especially large city and our paths may even have crossed unknowingly. They visited a home they knew to be the last residence my parents had lived in before they too left the city. The new owner knew my parents—knew me—but had no idea where any of us had gone. Another hope dashed.

CHAPTER 15

❀

My packing was almost complete. The mover had been booked and there were only the good-byes to attend to. Montreal was not the city I had moved to so many years earlier. All cities change with time, it is true, but somehow I didn't feel a part of the changes taking place in Montreal—we seemed to be growing in different directions. The compulsory use of the French language had grown more quickly than I was able to expand my vocabulary. I'm certain this played some part in my eventual realization that I no longer belonged there. After virtually a lifetime—marriage and a family grown—I began to feel more and more like a stranger. As much as I loved my apartment, it no longer felt like home.

My friends were all younger than I, and still working full time. They were occupied on evenings and weekends, just as we all had been at one time, catching up on things at home and making preparation for the week to come. Invariably, any association I joined for companionship began in English but ended up with the conversation reverting to French and this was not the language in which I could best communicate. A sense of loneliness began to pervade.

This thought process didn't take place over-night. The seed was planted somehow and then slowly it began to grow until one day there was the realization that I wanted to "go home". I had left my Southern Ontario home to escape from the ghosts of my past. Montreal had been good to me and had offered me sanctuary at a time when I was in desperate need. That exciting city had enabled me to get on with my life—allowing no time to grieve for my lost children. But finally I had stopped running. I realized I needed to go back to the beginning and to face the past squarely. It was the only way I could ever find closure and peace for myself.

My parents, of course, were no longer living. They had both died several years after they moved to British Columbia. My father had always claimed that was one place he wanted to see. They had no ties and their decision came easily—rather than simply visiting the place, they'd move there. Certainly the climate was more to my mother's liking. She couldn't stand the scorching summers in Southern Ontario and she was terrified of thunderstorms. Since Windsor is the thunderstorm capitol of North America, it's certainly not the place for someone with an aversion to them. In my younger days I had never understood her fear of storms. A storm to me meant a deluge of rain with lots of puddles left behind. I could hardly wait for the clouds to clear so I could scramble into my bathing suit and run outside to splash with abandon.

And now, I was down to virtually counting the hours before it was time for me to leave. Before I did, however, I wanted to put together a memory book for JM—a book similar to one I had made for Jacqueline on her previous birthday. It was a book containing scraps of information and photographs from my childhood and teen years, accompanied by the scant information I held concerning our family tree. I wanted my children to have some knowledge of the grandparents they had never really known. My mother had visited us briefly in Montreal on several occasions and we had been to visit her in Victoria, but this was after my father had died. Jacqueline was only a few weeks old when her grandfather came to see her and he died before JM was born.

As I sat contemplating what to write, my thoughts strayed to the branch of the family tree I couldn't include—John Albert, my first-born son and my long-lost daughter, Mary Margaret. That part of my life had remained a closed book that I didn't intend to open for anyone. Much as I thought Jacqueline and JM should know of their siblings, I hadn't yet found the strength to bring those hidden, painful memories into the open.

It was all I could do to avoid giving way to bitterness when I saw how much things had changed in fifty years. Unwed mothers were accepted in today's society. In fact I had worked with two who had purposely borne children because they wanted a family—but they had no wish to marry. They were allowed paid maternity leave on an equal basis with the married girls, and all the social programs including Medicare and Government Allowances were in place for them. By today's standards I could have kept my babies and remained an accepted member of society as well. The chances of us surviving financially would also have been very much in our favour. I didn't dare dwell on the aspects of the unfairness of it all—the "what might have been". What was done was done. Certainly it couldn't do me any good to dwell on it; nor could it serve any useful purpose.

In an attempt to rouse myself from the fruitless reverie, I began writing in JM's memory book. The first entry was my father's name and birth date, and then I began to pen my mother's name. It was difficult not to let my mind wander. My mother's name was only half formed on the page in front of me when I was suddenly jolted back to the present by the shrill sound of the telephone at my elbow:

"Hello?"

"I'm not sure I have the right number. I'm looking for a Ruth Watts." It was a male voice, and one I could not identify, but its engaging quality prompted my immediate response.

"Well, you've found her," I said cheerily.

The male voice continued, "Are you in a position to discuss a matter of a rather delicate nature?"

My mood shifted abruptly. This conversation was perhaps not the pleasant one that the voice had led me to anticipate. On guard now, I replied, "That all depends on what you wish to discuss."

"Albert Lester was your father?" he continued.

"Yes!"

At the sound of my father's name, all sense of caution vanished. I instinctively knew the caller's mission could only be something of interest—a link with the past, the long-ago past, which I had just been on the verge of revisiting. What a coincidence, I mused, and how curious that I had been thinking of my father only moments earlier.

The voice continued, "I was born May fourteenth, nineteen ..."

"Oh, my God!" I gasped as I felt the blood draining from my face, my heart pounding. "Oh, my God", I repeated again and again until at last I blurted out, "You have got to be the most often-thought-of person on the face of this universe!"

This can't be happening. This can't be—it's not real, I thought, and for a fleeting moment time stood still.

"Oh, man!" came the voice across the wire—a voice so filled with emotion there could be no doubt. It was real—this was really happening! I had never in my wildest dreams imagined such a moment! My thoughts began to race.

"Oh, man!" He repeated, and the sound of John's voice brought me back to the moment.

"How much do you remember?"

"Not enough," he replied.

A wave of relief swept over me with the realization that perhaps my years of self-recrimination and remorse, rooted in the circumstances under which we had parted fifty years earlier, had been wasted emotion. If he didn't remember, then perhaps he didn't hate me either, or at least harbour ill feeling toward me as I had always imagined. It was with some small sense of relief that I carried on the conversation, expressing a mixture of joy and disbelief that this was all really happening.

"Prepare yourself for another shock," John's voice continued, "I've met Mary Margaret."

"Mary Margaret!" How unprepared I was for this! I wanted to cry out—to know how he could possibly have met her. I gave her up at birth. How could he possibly know of her! What a cruel twist of fate. It was due to her existence that I felt I had to give them both up.

This was too much! There was no way I could control my racing thoughts now. I tried in vain to comprehend and to gain some semblance of composure. When finally I did respond, I could only say simply that I was not prepared to deal with her existence. I had given her up at birth, irrevocably and unequivocally.

How could I have ever envisioned future technology where computers would perform instantaneous matches of blood relatives with just one click? However, no amount of foresight could have prepared me for dealing with the subject of Mary Margaret again. I thought I had finally overcome the grief that overwhelmed me at our separation. In time, I had learned to stop wondering if she was walking yet. Was she talking? What did she look like now? Somehow I always imagined her with dark hair although John and their father were both blonde. I wondered if she was happy—and later, occasionally, I wondered if she was married—if she had children of her own. I had all but blotted her from my conscious mind—at least thoughts of her were less frequent and tortured. And now, to tear down all my defences—I was overwhelmed by the magnitude of it all, and suddenly felt so very vulnerable!

John and I talked for literally hours. How many hours I don't know because for me, that evening, time stood still. I had lost all awareness of time and place—as though I was suddenly in another dimension—and somehow removed from reality. I felt like I was dreaming but I knew I wasn't. I was wide awake and actually speaking with the son I had been parted from so many, many years ago!

When we finally hung up, there was no sleep for either of us. There was a need to reach out again—to reaffirm each other's existence—although we had already arranged to meet at the Toronto bus terminal on the twelfth of June on my stopover en route to my new home in Windsor.

John initiated the first of the subsequent e-mails a few hours later.

> "This is just too incredible! To suddenly have all the pieces of the puzzle fall together the way that they did seems so surreal. I am so very happy that my contacting you was welcomed. It is quite a moment ... one of the most significant of my life! I am still absorbing! Enclosed are a couple of pictures for you to play with between now and the twelfth. You know, I have been practicing what to say to you if I ever had the opportunity to actually talk to you—damned if I could remember any of it now! We have a tremendous amount of catching up to do, when you are ready. I sure hope that you will keep in touch during your move. I seem to have this fear of losing track of you again. Looking forward to actually seeing you very soon."

To which I responded:

> "Good morning ... and what a good morning it is! I thought I would sleep last night, but I didn't—hardly a wink, although I don't feel unrested this morning. I suppose we are both still in a state of shock to some extent! Thank you so very much for the pictures. I see a strong family resemblance. I thought of pictures I might send, but looking around this place I suddenly realize that to know which box they would be in is beyond me. I promise to take some and hopefully have them in time to send—if not I'll give them to you on the twelfth ... and no, you're not going to lose me again. I'm not going anywhere except to Windsor ... and that's a much smaller place to find people in! I'm looking forward to hearing from you and to our meeting on the twelfth! And now, to know how to sign myself off—what do you call me?"

This was followed several hours later with:

> "I couldn't sleep either. Yes, I am still in shock. I will do my best to hold on until the twelfth to see you face to face. I just cannot get over how, over-night, things have changed so dramatically. From two days ago when I had pretty much exhausted all hope of ever finding you, to making that chance enquiry re Albert and following up on the trail that led to you so quickly. It is all pretty astounding. Time enough to figure out what to call you. It really is a question of what is comfortable for you, and what feels natural. I am

just thankful to have the chance now to call you at all. What a wonderful new beginning."

It had been too late to call anyone after John and I had ended our telephone conversation the previous evening, so I had yet to tell Jacqueline and JM.

CHAPTER 16

❁

Jacqueline was already at the office by the time I called to tell her the wonderful news about John's phone call. I had just recently learned that she knew of John's existence—apparently her father had told her, much to my chagrin. I was adamant that it was my place to tell Jacqueline and JM about their siblings, and in my own way. However, before I had found the opportunity to do so, Jacqueline had confronted me on the subject. The conversation had taken place on one of her most recent visits to my apartment. Opening the old wounds quickly led to sobs on my part and our conversation on the subject had ended, unfinished, to be continued at a later date.

"How much does your brother know about John?" I asked when she finally came on the line.

"He knows of him but I have never told him about our conversation—why?"

After a brief pause I took a deep breath and said,

"Because John called me last night."

A resounding, "what?" was her retort, and then the questions came tumbling out one after the other before I had a chance to speak. I told Jacqueline all I could of the previous night's conversation and then agreed when she said she wanted to be the one to call JM to tell him the wonderful news. She was about to hang up when I said,

"Wait, there's more."

"You mean I have a sister too?" she quipped jokingly.

"Yes," I said, and now there was an even more resounding "what!"

Briefly, I told Jacqueline all I could about Cindy—as Mary Margaret was now known. By this time my fatigue was becoming obvious.

"Hang up, Mom, and let me digest this! I'll call JM—you go and get some rest."

A few hours later the phone calls began to fly back and forth with the big question being when they would get to meet their new brother—and sister. Both Jacqueline and JM expressed their happiness for me—delighted that my life had taken this miraculous turn, and also delighted to suddenly find themselves with the "older brother" they had often wished they had—and, for Jacqueline, the sister she had always longed for.

I informed them they might meet John sooner than they anticipated because, by this time, the two of us had decided that our arrangements for the twelfth seemed too far off. John had decided to fly to Montreal to crash the birthday dinner planned for me a few days later. He would fly up for the day and he and I could spend a few hours alone together in the afternoon. I tried to keep his visit as a surprise for Jacqueline and JM However, my clever daughter phoned my apartment not too long after John had arrived, and playfully demanded to speak to her brother.

The wait for John that afternoon was interminable. He called when his plane touched down at Dorval.

"I'm on my way," he said.

I tried to breathe. I couldn't. My chest felt constricted—my heart was pounding and my throat was dry. I felt as though my blood pressure had risen drastically and my pulse was racing. I began to fear that if he didn't soon arrive that I would not survive until he did. Relief, fear, and excitement—a gamut of many emotions surged through me and had reached their climax when the buzzer finally sounded. It was John, announcing that he was in the lobby.

I opened the door just as he reached the top of the stairs. There he was, directly in front of me. I would have known him anywhere! Finally, I was in his arms and he was once again in mine!

John had brought me three roses—one from him, one from his older brother Gordon, and one in Cindy's name although she didn't yet know that I had been found. Circumstances had prevented her from being told as yet, but John assured me that she was going to receive the bill for her rose as a means of letting her know she had not been excluded from the celebration of my birthday—knowingly or not. Accompanying the roses was a beautifully written birthday card from John—written from the heart and which to this day brings tears to my eyes.

"To my mother, Ruth. What does one say at a time like this? For as long as I can remember I have wondered if this incredible moment would ever arrive, and thought about what the most important thing might be that I would want to say to you. That one thing is … I understand.

It must not have been easy for you, all of those years, wondering if you had done the right thing. No one can tell what might have been had you not made that decision, but you need to know that, once it was made, my "new" family provided a safe, secure and enriching environment. My life has been full of opportunity and diversity. And yet, while nothing can replace the family that I have shared, you are the woman who gave me life and nothing will ever change that either. I am overjoyed that, at last, I am able to acknowledge this with you and to assure you that I recognize the courage that it must have taken for you to make that ultimate sacrifice. I have never seen this as a choice between right and wrong, just simply that you did what you thought was best. I hope that the kind of person that I have become will validate this for you in your heart.

Now life has brought us full circle, and for that I am thankful! What this new future holds remains to be seen, but I am hopeful that you will be a part of it with me."

Words cannot describe just how happy my birthday had turned out to be! Not only had I received the unbelievable gift of having John in my life once again—but he had also brought me a small album filled with copies of all his baby photos I had packed in that little shoebox and sent away with him. I had destroyed every remaining photo I had of him—but now, I had them all back again. That same afternoon I gave John my beloved box of Christmas tree lights. They had, after all, been his lights too. As much as they meant to me, and their connection with my father and my childhood, I hoped in some way they would bring John the same sense of continuity with his baby years.

As we talked that afternoon, John did his best to answer the question uppermost in my mind—how he had managed to find me? It appeared that, after years of searching, it was as simple as sitting down at his computer and searching cemetery records. Actually, he had done the same thing a couple of years earlier but had struck out. This time, he got a match. He found information regarding my father, and then the notice from the obituary column of a Victoria, British Columbia newspaper. John's heart leapt at the words, "also left to mourn, a daughter, Ruth (Mrs. Michael Watts) of Montreal."

He swung into action and immediately made a quick trip to the library to scan the Montreal telephone directory and found a listing for R.M. Watts. He had been told many years earlier that my first name was Ruth and, in his attempts to find me, had subsequently ascertained that my middle name was

Margaret. Elated and apprehensive at the same time, he wrote down the number and returned home to the privacy of his own telephone. There was nothing left to do but dial the number.

On his first attempt there was no answer, so he waited another hour and tried again. There was little doubt in his mind that he had found me after years of searching. One can only imagine what thoughts and mixed emotions ran through his mind during that hour, which must have seemed an eternity. John had steeled himself in the eventuality that I might reject him—I had no idea until later that so often this is the outcome. I can't conceive of such a thing, but I'm assured that statistics have proven this to be so.

I am still overwhelmed, and I suppose I always will be, when I think of the amount of courage it must have taken for him to make that call, knowing full well what a devastating outcome could have resulted.

I can only surmise how differently things could have turned out. In her will my mother had requested that there be immediate cremation—ashes to be disposed of, no ceremony and no publication. Had my father's wishes been similar to hers, it would have been yet another disappointment for John. The element of time was also involved. Had he made the call a couple of weeks later, I would have been gone. I would have moved back to the place where it had all begun and where he and Cindy had already searched with a fine-tooth comb. It's doubtful they would have retraced their steps in their search for me.

By the time Jacqueline and JM arrived at my apartment to meet their brother, John and I had caught up on so many things. We talked of the very few memories he had of toddler years with me—I was able to give him some photos of him that had been in my mother's possession. They'd been sent to me with some of her effects following her death. There was one of John taken with his Grandpa. All the other baby pictures John had were of him alone—they contain no identifiable places or people. Those had been confiscated.

John had also had time to explain to me that Cindy's adoptive mother was in the hospital, gravely ill. There was infection that would not heal, and it appeared that amputation of the leg was imminent which, in fact, turned out to be the only option that saved her life. John was very protective of his sister and felt that the news of having found me would be too much of a strain on Cindy in addition to all she was already going through. Her adoptive mother had long felt a deep rooted anxiety that I might be found one day and had worried that, should I reappear in Cindy's life, their relationship would not recover. Cindy had sought me out without her adoptive mother's blessing. She felt she had always been a good daughter, and would remain so, but owed it to her own children to investigate my background to determine any health issues that might be of importance to them. There was also her own peace of mind—a need to know what kind of person her birth mother really was.

What a joy to see the three children together at dinner that evening! Any fear John had that he might be seen as an intrusion into the lives of Jacqueline and JM was quickly dispelled. Jacqueline and JM were both thrilled to meet their older brother and their generosity of spirit quickly put John at ease. Jacqueline sat directly across from John at dinner and at one point remarked, "I'm looking into my mother's eyes." John does indeed have eyes like mine, something which neither Jacqueline nor JM have. Jacqueline has the appearance of being very like me although, for the most part, her features are different—it's her expression that has the similarity. She, like John, is fair with grey-blue eyes. JM has my dark curly hair and dark hazel eyes but mostly he resembles his father.

JM drove John to the airport to catch a ten o'clock flight and, filled with a sense of peace and well being, I went to bed anticipating my first good night's sleep in days. I went to bed reflecting on what a wonderful birthday this had turned out to be. I had received what was probably the most meaningful gift of my entire life—even if I live to be a hundred!

Sleep, however, did not come. The process of healing is a strange one. How could I have thought to assuage a virtual lifetime of denial in just the nine day's since John's call!

Tears began to flow and quickly they turned to sobs. I sobbed uncontrollably—deep, gut wrenching sobs—for what seemed like hours on end. I was totally unprepared for the catharsis I underwent that night. On and on it went until I thought surely my neighbours would hear me—and yet I could not stop. Exhausted, I finally slept only to wake a few hours later, cleansed at last.

Despite John's trip to Montreal, we still agreed to meet at the bus terminal in Toronto on the night of the twelfth—five days later. The movers emptied my apartment that day and my furniture was already en route to my new home. I was on my way to Windsor to be there in time to receive it.

CHAPTER 17

※

At the time of John's phone call I was in the midst of saying my goodbyes to Montreal and to all those near and dear to me. Some friends I had already said goodbye to before the momentous call. Others I was still scheduled to see, and I went to meet them armed with photos and a happy heart eager to tell them of the wondrous turn of events. My news, however, seemed to be met with mixed reactions. I had the feeling that long-time friends felt I had in some way betrayed them by not confiding in them. I did my best to explain that my former life had been a closed book—one to be buried in the mist of the past and not to be kept alive through disclosure. I had looked for acceptance as the person I am—not for understanding or sympathy for the person I had been.

I have attempted to remain in touch with those closest to me and I would hope, if indeed any feeling of betrayal exists on their part, that I am to be forgiven. It was never my intent to deceive. There was not sufficient time to truly explore their feelings before my imminent departure from the city.

The bus pulled in to the Toronto bus station half an hour early and I thought it a shame that John and I couldn't have known in advance and have had that extra time together—but there he was! John was already at the terminal and I saw him coming toward me from across the station. He had also arranged for his brother Gordon and Gordon's companion Adam to meet us there. When they arrived we went to the Second Cup for coffee and conversation—a most relaxed and enjoyable hour!

Gordon couldn't get over my references to my son JM—it turned out that John and Gordon also have a brother called JM. Just one more of the many coincidences! Gordon was also taken aback by my mannerisms—he could see Cindy in them. John had already told me that our voices are not dissimilar—only that hers is slightly higher than mine. Since John had first spoken to me, he had to ask on more than one occasion who the caller was since he was not certain whether it was Cindy or me. This was something that perplexed her until she became aware of the circumstances. Cindy had yet to be told about me.

The hour passed all too quickly and the three of them accompanied me out to the bus platform for goodbyes. While we waited in line a man approached us to enquire about buses. He told us he was on his way to meet his brand new grandson who was two days old. He expressed his excitement and asked if I was a grandmother and if so, how it felt when I became one. There was a burst of spontaneous laughter from the four of us as I said that I was indeed a grandmother and that it had come as a tremendous shock! I didn't elaborate but chose to leave him with the feeling that perhaps we had lost our sanity.

As it happened, Cindy had married her high school sweetheart, Gerald, and they were parents of Ryan and Elizabeth who were fully grown and finishing their post-secondary education. Furthermore, Elizabeth was to be married in a matter of months. Not only had I suddenly found myself to be a grandmother, but also I was on the brink perhaps of being a great-grandmother. A whole generation had escaped me—hence the shock!

Cindy, of course, was still in the dark as to John's discovery of me. Each time he went to visit Cindy and her seriously ill mother, I told him to "give Cindy a hug for me" and he had obliged. Cindy had noticed immediately that he was being more affectionate than usual and commented on the fact. It was a perfect introduction when it finally became time to broach the subject.

Meanwhile, I busied myself in my new home—the one I had found through my friend Fran's referral to an agent named Greg. I had written to Greg telling him of my requirements and then proceeded to wait for his response. Weeks turned into months and still no response. Somehow there had been a misunderstanding and Greg felt he would be unable to help me. My letter sat on his desk all the while pending his being able to come up with some sort of solution. As I was not arriving until the end of the summer, he felt no hurry to respond. Fran was livid and called him to complain bitterly. In short order I had a phone call and that began a series of e-mails through which we arranged an appointment for the day after the long Labour Day weekend. Through those e-mails I had begun to suspect that Greg was a caring and sincere individual and I began to think of him as a friend long before I finally met him.

The days of the immediate crisis with Cindy's mother had passed and Cindy was finally able to get some badly needed rest. John could contain himself no longer. He arranged to tell her the big news. He first phoned Cindy's husband, Gerald, at a time when he knew she would be out of earshot. Gerald was so happy to know that I had been found at long last. Apparently there was always the unspoken fear that by now, like their father, I too would be dead. They arranged for John to drive to their cottage in Muskoka the following day.

John began the introduction by producing some of the many photographs taken at my birthday dinner in Montreal. Very predictably, Cindy ran the gamut of emotion when realization finally dawned—from shock to joy, and then to anger at being excluded for so long. She felt particularly upset to learn that even Gordon and Adam had already met me before her. Finally, her emotions led to elation.

> "I was so relieved that Cindy finally knows!" I wrote to John. "It's so good to have the 'day of reckoning' over with and to know that we are now 'forthright and honest'—every time I think about us I start crying—happy tears, but nonetheless big wet tears and I can't talk. I tried to tell Greg that you had told Cindy and again started blubbering. He asked if she was happy about it and I told him you said it was a ten-Kleenex production. All for this time, I just had to let you know how very happy you have made me!"

There were hundreds of questions to be answered and much to be digested at the cottage that weekend. But, Cindy wrote the following letter to John on his return to Toronto the next evening, a copy of which he forwarded to me.

> "Although I am very tired, I cannot go to sleep. My mind is racing ... I want so much to tell people about you finding our mother.
>
> Oh, John, I just can't tell you how I have longed for this moment and prayed that it would happen. My heart is absolutely bursting with joy to see the peace and happiness this has brought to you. It is very evident from seeing the pictures that you have brought the same joy and peace to Ruth. Although I have not experienced it personally yet, as a mother and an adopted child I can understand what a reunion of this type means to both of you. It is a profound experience filled with overwhelming emotions. To think that I am about to share the same experience is a dream come true ... truly another miracle! The happiness I feel cannot be put into words. I just pray that this dream becomes a reality very soon. I just don't want Ruth to be afraid.
>
> I have looked at the pictures over and over again. She is so beautiful and lovely. I try to imagine the sound of her voice, her laugh, her mannerisms ... what it will feel like to hug her. I especially love the pictures of you together and can't help but be excited and thrilled to think that, one day

soon, there will be pictures of the three of us together. and then with our brother and sister too! This is all so incredibly wonderful.

I have tried to write a letter to Ruth a few times tonight. I just keep staring at the screen not knowing where to start and what to say. I want to find just the right words but can't seem to get down on paper what I feel in my heart. This is so important. I can only imagine what she is going through right now and how difficult coming to terms with my presence must be. I don't want the letter to be too much too soon for fear of overwhelming her and yet it is hard for me to be anything other than emotional. I will keep trying. I do want her to know that I feel no resentment whatsoever and that I know she did what she had to do and what she thought best for us, and it was done out of love.

Well, your e-mail just arrived. Thank you for sharing part of what Mom said. I wasn't going to tell you but now I will … I have been crying too ever since you left. They are also tears of joy that just won't stop. Oh, John, this is really happening. Isn't it? She is real! I desperately want and need to have contact with her too. Did she say anything more about when she might be ready to talk to me or to meet me? You know I will respect her wishes, but I was just wondering if you had any idea. I must try to write the letter. I want her to know how I feel. I am just so afraid of making a mistake.

I can barely see the letters on my keyboard anymore through all the tears so I guess it is time for me to say goodnight. I am so happy you were here this weekend. I just wish you were still here. I could use one of your extra special hugs right now. I love you too."

When I had finished reading Cindy's message to her brother, the resistance of all the years melted away in an instant. I once again allowed myself to feel the pain I had experienced when I signed her adoption papers and let her go from my arms into the arms of her foster mother. I felt the grief I had denied myself at the time and with it came the healing and the joyful realization that I could once again see her and hold her. There was no longer any need to go slowly. As soon as she was able to leave her mother's bedside, I was more than ready to meet her and I immediately wrote John to tell him so!

"I was deeply moved by Cindy's lovely letter. The tears still flow each time I re-read it. I do long to see her and I hope it will be soon! At the moment I seem to alternate between tears and fatigue. I had my nap, as promised, but was sorely in need of another within the hour … I'm not going to go on at length—I can't. Tell Cindy that there is no need to write to me … her letter to you has said it all. I love you both, dearly."

Our meeting finally took place on the fourteenth of July, just thirty-seven days after my reunion with John—and forty-six days following his momentous phone call. John outdid himself in arranging the meeting and, although we had discussed several ways of going about it, in the end it was decided that neutral ground for a brief initial visit was best.

John arranged for a suite at a hotel in the neighbourhood in which I had grown up. Cindy was given a room on the same floor as the suite where we were to meet at last. They arrived on a Friday evening and, very early Saturday morning, John came to pick me up. He had arranged a continental breakfast to be served in the suite.

I was more than ready for coffee by that time for I had, much to my chagrin, wakened that morning with what appeared to be a hangover. I would never have believed it possible. Greg had very thoughtfully called the previous evening. He knew I'd be in a terribly anxious state. He brought over some mussels to cook and I had some salmon in the freezer. It was a delicious meal but I was unable to manage more than a few mussels and a mouthful or two of salmon, following our pre-dinner drink. I was unable to sleep that night either. The lack of food and sleep seemed to triple the effect of the small amount of alcohol I'd consumed, and the resulting headache did nothing to soothe my nerves.

When we entered the suite my eyes fell upon a huge bouquet of beautiful white roses. I later discovered they were mine—a gift from Cindy and John. Later we took a lovely photo of Cindy holding them. It's one of my favourite pictures.

Once we were settled, John went down the hall to get Cindy and, just as I had felt overly emotional when I waited for John's arrival from the airport in Montreal, once again I had the feeling I might not survive even those few moments that it took until Cindy arrived.

Finally, the door opened and Cindy entered the room. I had been standing looking blankly out of the window. I turned to the centre of the room facing the door as she entered. Our eyes met briefly before her hands flew to her face. Suddenly there was no space between us and we clung to each other, both of us trying desperately not to let our tears give way to sobs. So many tears had already been shed and there was so much catching up to do! Finally, Cindy whispered, "Are you all right?" I replied, "Yes, are you?"

We stood back and looked at each other. Then we sat down and looked at each other—we couldn't stop looking at each other. We became embarrassed when we realized we were actually staring at each other. Cindy's similarity to me was incredible, right down to the smallest details. Cindy has my dark hair, my eyes, my hands and fingers. We're the same height and build, unlike my daughter Jacqueline who towers over me. Cindy even seemed to have inherited my weakness for losing my voice when I become overtired or stressed—she couldn't speak above a whisper.

Cindy had brought pictures of her family to show me, and gave me a copy of my high school yearbook that she had obtained on one of her expeditions in search of me. I was thrilled to have that treasure trove of memories. One of the first things I noticed was the page of names of boys and girls who had made the ultimate sacrifice during the war—my sweetheart's name was among them. My pictures were in there too—one as a member of the gym team, and another taken on the annual day when our school took over Smith's Department store. It was a copy of the newspaper photo in which I was pictured selling toiletries to the school principal.

Some months before our reunion, John and Cindy had used one of those pictures to create a portrait of me that stands on the mantle, in clear view, in one of their group pictures taken one Christmas. It was incredible to me that they had such longing to include their unknown mother in their lives—long before they knew whether or not they would ever find me.

It had been such a long haul of tense anticipation for all of us. We agreed to part company to catch a few hours rest before meeting later for a celebratory dinner. On the way back to my home, I took John past the house where I grew up, which he in turn was able to point out to Cindy on their way to pick me up for dinner that evening.

We ate downtown at Joseph's. The meal was delicious and exquisitely presented—a perfect cap to a perfect reunion. We were aware of a sense of belonging to one another. There was no strangeness among us. By the time the evening was through, John was calling Cindy "the clone". He told us it was "scary" to watch Cindy and me together. We struck similar poses as we sat, and when walking together we had the same gait. John had already realized before Cindy and I met that there was a great deal of similarity between us, but even he had not been prepared for the reality

After dinner we went to the nearby Casino but lady luck did not smile on us. No one was disappointed because we were already the wealthiest people on earth in our estimation. When we said goodnight and parted, Cindy gave me a framed copy of her favourite photograph of John and her. It now stands with other family photos on a side table in my bedroom—a treasured memento of that very special day.

CHAPTER 18

❀

There were still other reunions to be arranged. I still had not met either my grandchildren or Gerald, Cindy's husband. Cindy was anxious to meet Jacqueline and JM, her newly discovered brother and sister. They, in turn, were just as anxious to meet her. John, of course, had met the two of them when he made the memorable trip to Montreal for our reunion.

A time and place for the four siblings to meet was top priority. I was eager also to have my friends meet my "new" son and daughter—friends with whom I had shared my news and who had been so wonderfully supportive. They shared my joy. Since Cindy's good friend, Anita, and I lived in the same city—as did my long-time friends Fran, Bob, and also Greg, my home seemed to be the logical place to congregate despite the fact that many of my belongings were still relegated to their original packing cases. I had brought far more with me than my new home could accommodate. Weeding out the items I'd need to dispense with would prove to take a considerable amount of time—far more time than we could afford at the moment. The upcoming Labour Day weekend appeared to be the favoured time for the momentous occasion when we would finally become a family united.

Although I was exhausted from all the preparation, I was borne up by my excitement. We were going to celebrate at a Sunday brunch. I baked cakes that I had not attempted in more than twenty years, and prepared many side dishes to serve along with the smoked salmon, cream cheese and the real Montreal bagels I had asked Jacqueline to bring. John, Cindy and I went shopping for some last-minute items on Saturday afternoon and returned in time to await the arrival of Jacqueline and JM who were driving down from Montreal.

Time seemed to go so slowly. Once again there was that "first meeting" tension. Both Jacqueline and Cindy give easily to tears, and I was bracing myself for an encounter where they would end up being overly emotional because that would surely set me off. I was already having a problem holding my own emotions in check.

Eventually they arrived and Jacqueline burst into my front hall in such a dishevelled state from the lengthy car trip that there was more laughter than tears, and in a moment it was as though they had known one another forever. Jacqueline's first reaction upon seeing Cindy was to blurt out—"and I thought I looked like my mother!"

The conversation was animated and continuous and I was so happy to just sit back and watch. There is no way to express the full extent of my emotion, and what that moment meant to me. It was something I could never have dared to imagine. My four children and I were together!

The numbers for my Sunday brunch grew, but that wasn't a problem as there was plenty of food. In my usual fashion, concern there would not be enough had led to the end result of there being far too much. Anita's mother accompanied her, as did Anita's daughter and son-in-law. John's brother Gordon drove from Toronto to be with us, and my friends Bob and Fran came—and Greg, of course.

The brunch seemed to go successfully and everyone was lavish with their compliments about the food I had prepared. It didn't appear, either, that anyone minded the unpacked boxes of books that seemed to occupy every unused corner of the living room. I might have moved them to a less conspicuous area had not every nook and cranny throughout the entire house already been filled beyond capacity! I was so grateful that the gathering seemed to be a success, regardless, but it meant so much more to me to have my friends meet my children—and to have them meet my friends. Fran came to the kitchen while the gathering was in progress and said simply, "These are all such nice people." I could only agree, wholeheartedly.

In the evening we met again for another celebratory dinner at a charming restaurant—Brigantino's. It was interesting to see how the four siblings naturally gravitated to one end of the long table while the rest of us were arranged at the other end. It was their special weekend and they were making the most of it.

All too soon the weekend was over and it was time for emotional goodbyes. Only physical distance would separate us now—family bonds had been formed and bound us closely together. Before going back to Toronto the next day, John's brother Gordon stopped in for a brief visit and I was so pleased that the two of us had the opportunity to get to know each other better. On the way home Gordon very thoughtfully stopped and sent a gorgeous bouquet of flowers with a note that read, "What a wonderful party." It had indeed been wonderful. Now to overcome the disbelief that this has all really happened!

Cindy's family had been unable to attend the siblings' reunion so there still remained a time and place for me to meet Gerald, my son-in-law, and Elizabeth and Ryan, my grandchildren. I was finding it easier to say the word "grandchildren". I had never given much thought to it before and, most certainly, had never been disappointed that neither Jacqueline nor JM had married and had children. The memory of the active little girl I had raised always prompted me to jokingly tell Jacqueline that the day she became a mother I would start out on a trip around the world. Now, suddenly, the word grandmother took on a new depth of meaning.

I gave John my father's wristwatch during the reunion weekend. My father is wearing that watch and it is visible in the picture I gave John the first day we met—a photo of the two of them that had been among my mother's possessions. I also gave him a card, written in response to his beautifully written birthday card to me the day we met. I wrote:

> "To John, my son—my son! How many years has it been since I have dared to utter those words whenever thoughts of you crossed my mind, and how many years has it been that I have tried in vain to deny entry to those thoughts. You were my first born, the baby I had longed for from earliest childhood. A lifetime of desire, every cherished dream came into being in you. My decision was the only course, but one that my heart has never been able to accept as "right". Pangs of remorse and guilt have been my constant companions. Whatever I have done to deserve your love at this point in my life, I can only thank God for all His goodness and hope and pray that we will go forward from here—together once again! Your mother, Ruth."

With John's first phone call my life began yet again There is not only the unbelievable reality that I am reunited with my two lost children but, at the same time, I have found still more happiness in the form of my dear friend Greg, who inspires in me the same depth of feeling I had thought it impossible to ever recapture.

It was as simple as opening a door. Greg was to pick me up at Fran's house. It was the appointment we had arranged during his original phone call to me in Montreal. We were embarking on a whirlwind mission to find me a suitable home within the next three days. I ran in response to the sound of the bell, and threw open the door with the casual greeting, "Hi, Greg, I'm Ruth." It was a far cry from my fleeting thoughts as I caught my first glimpse of him and looked into his eyes.

Somewhere, deep within, I felt a sense of great relief. My innermost thoughts seemed to say, "At last you're here—I've been waiting so very long for you!" There was no question and no surprise at my reaction. For the second time in my life I felt that it was a perfectly normal response to someone who could only be a soul mate—so familiar was he to me! I cannot aptly describe the emotion—only that something long forgotten had been rekindled. Somewhere in the deep recesses of my heart I had found that it was not impossible to re-visit the wonderment of a first love. I have been doubly blessed.

There are moments when I still believe I may awake and find this has all been but a dream. In truth, it is a dream—a dream come true.

Epilogue

※

Time has passed since the writing of this book began and there have been many changes in our lives—engagements, marriages and, sadly, some deaths.

There have been more reunions as well. One in particular, hosted by Gordon, saw the whole family and many of their friends mingle for an enjoyable afternoon on a gorgeous sunny day on the grounds surrounding his beautiful swimming pool. It was there that I finally met my grandchildren, Elizabeth and Ryan. Both have since married, and Elizabeth is now the mother of a beautiful baby daughter. I had spent years unaware that I was a grandmother, and I'm ecstatic now to actually experience the thrill of being a great grandmother.

There was a moment of good humoured laughter when, upon his introduction to me, Ryan exclaimed, "You look just like my mother". The fact that Cindy resembles me did not go unnoticed in more than one instance that afternoon. Upon his arrival at the party, my friend Ronald encountered Cindy and stopped so abruptly in his tracks that Cindy later said she thought she might have caused him to have a heart attack. For his part, Ronald said he thought for a moment he had stepped into a time warp.

We are a family and, though sometimes still astounded by the wonderment of it all, it is difficult to remember a time when it was not so. Jacqueline and JM readily embraced the fact of another brother and another sister and, having accepted that fact, their lives continued on as though this is how it had always been—scarcely missing a beat. For Cindy and for John it has been much more profound—just as it has been for me—to have some fifty years of aching separation suddenly vanish. Our lives have been changed dramatically forever.

Greg has revealed himself to be the man I recognized deep within his eyes at the moment of our first meeting. My love grows with each passing year. It's difficult for me to recall now how it was before Greg entered my life as well. Perhaps what might be of equal importance is the fact that I have found the courage to reveal myself to him.

During my treatment for depression, layer upon layer of a lifetime of built-up defences were stripped away. I learned that all my flaws and my shortcomings were existent in everyone. They are more pronounced in some than in others, of course, but the capability is there in all of us by simple virtue of the fact we are all human. I learned that, although I was uniquely me, I wasn't "different". I had a newly found feeling of kinship with my fellow man and this knowledge gave me the strength to relate to those around me more openly. But I had not yet found myself in the position of wanting to bare the very essence of my soul to anyone. Whatever it was that I saw in Greg's eyes at that first moment of meeting, it gave me the strength and the desire to reveal my vulnerabilities without reservation. I have made the amazing discovery that I am loved for the person I truly am. What a blessing to finally learn that perfection is not a prerequisite to being accepted and loved.

I have discovered a peace that I never before knew could exist. I no longer feel compelled to keep moving in search of an elusive happiness—or to run from my fear of past ghosts. There are no ghosts—they have all become a wondrous reality. I know now what true happiness is. Contentment has become second nature to me and I am fulfilled.

Ruth

Conclusion

❧

So there you have it. Ruth's story of her earlier years is the story of thousands of women in this country. But it has a remarkably happier ending than statistics would suggest.

Ruth made the best decision she could under enormously difficult circumstances. Since being found by John and Cindy, she has realized some peace of mind knowing that she made the right decision. Both children were raised by decent people in good environments. The two were provided with many opportunities they would not have enjoyed had Ruth raised them without the array of social supports that exist in this century.

In my teaching, I make the point to my students that life can be summed up as follows: in the first eighteen or twenty years of life, a whole lot of things happen to you, and you then spend the rest of your life sorting that out.

It sounds a bit facetious, of course, but in reality the patterns of one's life are generally set in childhood. It takes many years to see some of the influences that subconsciously affect and guide us, and sometimes it takes a long time to understand the cause-and-effect in one's life. But we have to see and understand these influences in order to work through them and take control of our lives. We achieve different degrees of success in each of these aspects of our experiences, of course, but we rarely stop striving throughout our years to understand ourselves.

But adopting a child has an impact not just on the birth parents and the adoptive parents. The arrival of an adopted child ripples through the immediate and extended families, as well as friends, associates and members of the community. I watched this happen in my own family not once but four times over.

Growing up in a family with four adopted children—two as siblings and two as cousins—yet being part of the traditional married family-with-two-biological children, I had a different outlook on life than my friends whose brothers and sisters were all birth siblings.

For one thing, I read everything I ever came across about adoption: stories of children seeking birth family members, stories of mothers who had given their children up for adoption, stories of people whose lives were positively or negatively affected by adopted children seeking their birth families.

I read them all voraciously. But I never encountered an article about a sibling whose adopted brother or sister wanted to find their birth family. I've had a very interesting perspective in recent years, and it is this experience which I bring to Ruth's Epilogue.

When my adopted brother and sister were younger, they seemed disinterested in learning anything about their birth families. Yet when they both approached 40 years of age—or thereabouts—issues about biological medical histories began to invade their thinking. By this stage our father had died and our mother, as it turned out, was in the closing years of her life.

When John signed on with the Adoption Disclosure Agency, he was stunned to discover he had a full birth sister. We had been told he was an only child and naturally accepted that fact. At first we were excited at the prospect John had a sister. The challenge became, "How to find her?" It was heartbreaking to watch him put birthday greetings in many Ontario papers on his sister's birth date—only to come up with no response.

We now know that Cindy—though she knew she was adopted—had no idea she had a birth brother so she would not have paid attention to the notice even if she had encountered it.

When my adopted sister Anne decided she needed to learn something about her biological family, she flew east from British Columbia where she lived to spend a couple of weeks with me. She asked me to drive her 150 kilometres to London, Ontario, where she could sign on with the Adoption Disclosure Agency, too. Anne was nervous at the prospect of driving there because she worried that she might become too emotionally upset afterwards to be able to drive back to my home with any degree of safety. So we set out together to initiate her quest.

In time Anne was connected with three birth sisters but, unfortunately, they tried to change her into someone else. Anne never did react well to any smothering in her life so when her sisters began to press emotional buttons, she backed away and left a great deal of space between her and them.

And that is fine, too, since she has accepted that reality.

Growing up with adopted siblings made me aware of a host of issues that I doubt would have entered my thinking had my childhood been completely "traditional". And it is these issues that I never saw discussed in the articles I'd read throughout my life—from the perspective of an adoptee's brother, that is.

Some of the first words I ever spoke to Cindy shortly after she and John first met several years ago were to assure her that, had my parents Faye and William still been alive, they would have been the first people on the doorstep welcoming Cindy into our family.

Two years later when John and Cindy found their birth mother, I repeated the same sentiment to Ruth.

Few things would have given my parents more pleasure than to see a broken circle repaired. They were never threatened by the idea that one day in the future the adopted children in our family might want to find their birth family. I remember them saying on many occasions that they would do everything they could to help John and Anne with their journey should that day come. They never forced the issue; they simply acknowledged that such might be the case one day.

So what did growing up in a family of six children from five different biological bloodlines mean for me? I've often puzzled over its influences.

Certainly one of the things it taught me was to question the moral code that my Presbyterian religion proclaimed when I was dutifully attending church throughout my childhood. The hypocrisy I encountered about many social issues confused me greatly and, of course, ultimately led to my leaving the Presbyterian Church. Judgmentalism has never appealed to me, for I've always seen life as being made up of thousands of shades of grey rather than absolute black-and-white.

I couldn't accept the meanings of harsh, absolute words used in debates involving morality. Think of the word "bastard" for example. From my earliest understanding of the concept, I failed to see why someone should be shunned for having a child out of wedlock and I certainly couldn't accept the word "bastard" for such a child.

I was delighted when I first encountered the terms "love child" and "natural child" because the words themselves shed any moral judgment. They replace negativity with positivism.

In time, this led to a belief that marriage should be viewed as a state of mind rather than a legal status.

My adopted sister Anne came from a dysfunctional family where both parents were in and out of the sociological-legal system for many years before the children of that marriage were split up and placed in various orphanages and foster homes. Anne confided in me many decades later that she had actually lived in every orphanage in London, Ontario, at one point or other before she came to live with us in Woodstock.

How did her parents' marriage bring any special state of grace to Anne? I know many couples who live together without benefit of clergy whose emotional commitment is pure, and whose relationship supports children of loving and generous nature.

In studying history, I learned that marriage has evolved over many centuries and every society has created its own rules. A century ago one had to be Anglican to be legally married in Ontario. Marriage between blacks and whites only became legal in the USA in the 1960's. In the days of William Shakespeare, marriage ceremonies as we understand them were reserved for the aristocracy but peasants married simply by declaring their intention in front of witnesses. I learned there are no absolutes in terms of marriage and morality. Even so-called eternal truths of major organized religions evolved over millennia—misogyny, slavery, patriarchal structures have all been subject to evolutionary thought.

Perhaps, I then mused, we must make sense of our individual journey in life.

In time, I learned that the gay and lesbian movement describe us all as having two families: our birth family and our family of choice. We have no control over who our birth family happens to be, but we gather around us during life a group of people who become our family of choice. Sometimes—if we are lucky, *really* lucky—our family of choice includes most of our birth family.

But the two do not necessarily overlap. In fact, more often than not they are dissimilar. Chaos occurs when birth families insist they must be the family of choice, too!

Society is filled with people whose birth families have raised, but not accepted, one or more offspring: their children marry someone the parents/grandparents/siblings don't approve of. Perhaps the son or daughter chooses to live with someone instead of marrying them. Or they fail to achieve academic benchmarks. Perhaps their careers don't meet the family's expectations. There are as many reasons for disappointment as there are family units on the face of the earth.

I suppose there are just as many children who are disappointed that their parents don't live up to their expectations, either.

In reality, we are each dealt a hand of cards to play in life, and it is how we play them that truly matters.

As for my family—John's adoptive family—we had our own set of parameters. Part of my mother's side of the family was highly judgmental in its view of "the world". I had a grandparent who wouldn't allow unmarried couples to share a bedroom at the cottage—despite the fact my friends had been living together for nearly a decade. Yet my father's family line seemed entirely more relaxed on the subject of public morality—though not personal morality; they had high standards there. The Lewis side of my family was determined to accept everyone on the basis of their character, not their circumstances.

It took a lot of time to resolve the discrepancy in values that were presented to me as a child. I used to tease my mother that I would put on her tombstone, "But What Would the Neighbours Say?" It seemed to be the basis on which she formed so many opinions.

Here is the classic example of what I mean. When I finished university, I moved back to my family home for a while. One day while I was alone, I received a phone call from a friend who had given birth a few weeks earlier to a child born out of wedlock. We had been friends all the way through school and university, we had gone to the same church, and she had been through this overwhelming experience alone; she was too full of shame to contact any of her friends. I had heard via the grapevine of what had happened, but I had not even spoken to her because (as I knew) she did not want anyone to know what was happening in her life. Immediately I invited my friend to lunch.

When I told my mother that my friend was going to join me for lunch at home, my mother's reaction was based on concern that there would be no chaperone present. This was the mid-sixties in small-town Ontario, after all. But my father's reaction was one hundred per cent opposite: invite her to lunch and damn what anybody has to say. She's your friend and it's nobody else's business—including my parents. If ever I had a blinding example in my life of what Ruth and John and Cindy and the entire cast of characters had to deal with—it arrived there and then. Lunch was delicious—and my friend and I talked for hours.

So there you have it, yet again. Ruth's story. John's story. Cindy's story. My story. I hope you enjoyed it. But never stop thinking it through …

Gordon Lewis

978-0-595-46835-5
0-595-46835-7

Printed in the United States
87786LV00003B/319-333/A

9 780595 468355